ALEC CLIFTON-TAYLOR   SIX ENGLISH TOWNS

ALEC CLIFTON-TAYLOR

SIX ENGLISH TOWNS

BRITISH BROADCASTING CORPORATION

Published by BBC Publications
a division of BBC Enterprises Ltd
35 Marylebone High Street
London WIM 4AA

ISBN 0 563 20490 7

First published 1978
Text revised and printed as six
separate paperbacks 1984
Complete paperback edition,
incorporating text revisions,
first published 1986, reprinted 1986

Printed in England by
Jolly & Barber Limited
Rugby, Warwickshire

Title page illustration: Ludlow from Whitcliffe

CONTENTS

photographs by Geoff Howard

FOR

ROBERT STORRAR

WITH WHOM

THROUGH FORTY YEARS OF FRIENDSHIP

I HAVE LOOKED

AT MANY OLD ENGLISH TOWNS

NOT TO MENTION

OVER TWO THOUSAND CHURCHES

INTRODUCTION

Six English towns: yes, but why only *six*, when the good ones number at least a hundred? The question is very pertinent. The answer is that this book originated in a series of television programmes made throughout 1977 and first screened in 1978. Six was the number of towns which the BBC invited me to choose; and I still vividly remember that the task of selection involved three of us, Bruce Norman, the executive producer, Denis Moriarty, the producer, and myself, in a whole day of pleasurable deliberation. There were so many candidates that seemed to be positively crying out to be included!

We simplified our problem a little by imposing upon ourselves certain limitations. We decided to opt for fairly small towns, which could be explored within the compass of a single programme, and we needed places where the volume of traffic did not make filming impossible. In the event, we had many other factors with which to contend besides the traffic. Sun going in, film running out, dogs barking, children squeaking, aeroplanes roaring, pedestrians yearning to be photographed; even a speck of dust in the camera, rendering necessary a complete retake of more than one sequence.

Then, of course (for this was the BBC), as soon as we had chosen a town in the South we (very properly) had to have one in the North – or vice versa. Balance: between classical architecture and romantic, between planned towns and unplanned, between flat sites and hilly sites, between grey stone and red brick. Oh yes, and, although it certainly must not dominate the treatment, even when (as quite often) it was the town's *raison d'être*, it would be good, if possible, to include a 'big bang' – an abbey or cathedral, a castle or a mansion, as well as a place of high average quality architecturally.

Nor was there any thought of devising 'guided tours'. You will search in vain here for details about places where the first Queen Elizabeth is supposed to have slept, or where Keats wrote – well, whatever he did write there, or where Cowper or Housman or whoever is your favourite poet lies buried in the churchyard. There is nothing, either, about places famous for annual junketings of immemorial antiquity, like Abbots Bromley, with its fantastic reindeer's horn dance, or Dunmow with its flitch of bacon, which any couple might go to claim if they were prepared to swear, before the prior, the convent and the assembled townspeople, that for a year and a day, sleeping or waking, they had not repented of their marriage. Rather was it the intention that each programme should be a kind of exercise in looking. So we wanted towns of character; for with towns, as with people, if what you are seeking is a positive impact, you go for the place with a strong, decided personality.

We were specially interested in contrasts of colour and texture: and that means traditional building materials, which have long been a particular interest of mine: they, indeed, were the subject of my first book, *The Pattern of English Building*, which originally appeared as long ago as 1962. Stone, of many kinds and ages; brick, varying a good deal from place to place; wood, so abundant in England in earlier days; plaster, to which colour might or might not be added: all these have a long and honourable history. Until the advent of the railways, people usually built with what lay most conveniently to hand; only the Church and a few grandees could afford to use anything else. This was visually extremely fortunate, for it meant that every building looked right in its own locality. So strong were these local traditions, based primarily upon materials, that anyone who has been about a good deal, particularly in the stone areas, will presently find that the whereabouts of a town or a village, provided that it has not been much altered since 1850, can usually be pinpointed from photographs with a fair degree of accuracy. For there can be few parts of the world, if indeed any, in which so many kinds of stone have been available to builders within so small a compass. Visually, this has been one of England's greatest pieces of good luck; and the fact that so few people can afford to use stone today, and that, if they can, the range of choice is now so limited, has been a great misfortune for the art of architecture.

Virtually every English town started life with all, or nearly all, its houses built either with a timber framework or, in some areas, of mud. Needless to say, scarcely any medieval town houses in these materials have survived. But even where stone was readily available, wood, which was usually also very easy to procure, was preferred, because it was so much cheaper. The infilling was wattle and daub; later lath and plaster, or, still later, brick nogging. Small stone houses in the Middle Ages were a rarity. It was from about 1570 that, in places where stone was at hand locally, wood started gradually to be replaced; but the process was very slow, and a hundred years later the majority of English towns were still largely timber-framed. In the eighteenth century almost everyone who could not afford to rebuild would give their old house a smart new front in brick or stone, but often the timber-framing can still be seen at the back.

It was in the later seventeenth and especially in the eighteenth century that stone and brick really came into their own for town houses. Timber framing was in any case quite unsuited to the classical style, which was now universally preferred. Town fires were all too frequent, and wherever they occurred timber-framing and thatched roofs were prohibited in the rebuilding. Thus there came into being that gracious Georgian architecture which figures prominently in this book. In my opinion we have never at any other time designed and built town houses as good to look at as these. And in their mastery over materials – stone, brick, wood, iron, plaster: these in particular – the Georgian builders have never been surpassed. It seems inevitable that in all these six towns the Georgian buildings should be highlighted.

A main object both of the television programmes and of this book was and is to give pleasure. For that reason, very little attention has been devoted to what has been built since about 1850. Would that it could have been otherwise! It has been a continual sadness to me to find myself, in architecture, so out of sympathy with my own time; but the causes are largely economic. There are, I do not doubt, many architects who would be delighted to build with the traditional materials, especially stone, if only it were financially possible to do so. There are others, it is true, who seem to enjoy erecting high-rise buildings at the expense of the luckless towns whose visual identity is destroyed by these detestable intruders; no such desecrated town, of course, figures in this book. All the towns discussed here, in their historic parts at least, have now been designated under the Civic Amenities Act of 1967 as Conservation Areas: Stamford, indeed, was first to the post in all England in this respect. So there is a good chance that their future preservation will be secure; let us hope so. For that Act of Parliament is, to date, without doubt the most effective piece of legislation in defence of our old towns, and its powers should be used to the full. Happily, it is evident that in every one of these towns there is at least a *cadre* of people anxious to do just this. Nothing was more heartening, during the work of preparing the television programmes, than the generous scale of the help freely and even eagerly given by local people, several of them retired schoolmasters, unselfishly devoted to the subject of their town's future. In this body of good will and loving concern the cause of conservation certainly has one of its most precious assets.

For such towns as these, the lessons for the future are clear and obvious. No widening of streets in the older parts but, on the contrary, increasing pedestrian precincts; no multi-storey car parks (although the ample provision of parking places, tactfully sited, is of course essential); no high-rise buildings impinging upon the skyline; and the sympathetic use of materials. No large slabs of exposed concrete should ever be allowed where stone and brick prevail, for concrete, though a wonderful material structurally, does not weather nor grow mellow: it merely cracks, stains, and becomes shabby and finally sluttish-looking.

In the chapters which follow, an effort has been made to capture something of the flavour of each of the six towns that were ultimately selected for study. Nobody could be more aware than I of the many omissions. To try to 'put over' a town of the quality of, say, Chichester in a half-hour television programme might well be regarded as rash, if not presumptuous. So I hope that it will be clearly understood that these are not systematic descriptions; they are no more than an attempt to present what I have felt to be each town's essential quality, to come to grips with the very stuff out of which its buildings have been fashioned, and to indicate some of the features to look out for. The follow-up must be left to each individual reader; and, if he cares for architecture, he should have half a dozen considerable treats ahead of him.

All six towns – six towns which, by the way, until the Second Reform Bill of 1867 all had two Members of Parliament – are small enough to get to know intimately, just by walking about. They all exercise a strong appeal for their architectural qualities and for their range of building materials, and it goes without saying that special vigilance is needed to see that no one is allowed to damage or despoil places as good as these. Yet they are in no sense museums. They are working towns: and this is what I like to see. Working towns, which are none the less part and parcel of the great English heritage.

CHICHESTER

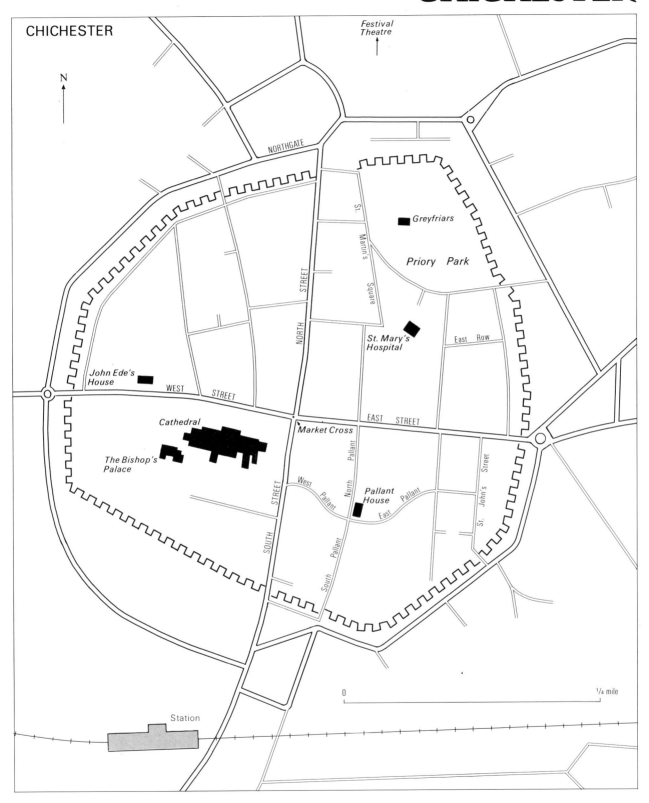

CHICHESTER

N

Festival Theatre

NORTHGATE

St. Martin's Square

Greyfriars

Priory Park

St. Mary's Hospital

East Row

NORTH STREET

John Ede's House

WEST STREET

Cathedral

The Bishop's Palace

Market Cross

EAST STREET

North Pallant

West Pallant

East Pallant

Pallant House

St. John's Street

SOUTH STREET

South Pallant

0   ¼ mile

Station

1. *Chichester – town plan*

2. *Chichester from the north-east*

Of my six towns, Chichester is the oldest: the only one with important Roman associations. Indeed, it was founded before the arrival of the Romans.

On the South Downs some five miles north of Chichester, just above Goodwood racecourse, there is a circular early Iron Age fort known as the Trundel. (The word *tryndel* meant a circle in Old English.) It seems very probable that it was from here, early in the first century BC, that a people known as the Regni came down off the chalk into the much more fertile plain, to establish at Chichester (as it is now called) their first tribal capital. The Romans first arrived in Sussex in AD 43. From the outset the inhabitants collaborated, so there was no fighting. The king of the Regni, Cogidubnus, was given Roman citizenship and left in charge here, as a sort of *gauleiter*.

The principal relic of the Roman period is not in Chichester itself but at Fishbourne, a mile and a half to the west. Fishbourne only started to yield its secrets in 1960, and parts of it lie under the main road to Portsmouth and under much later buildings. But it clearly began as a military establishment: it is on the shore of Chichester Harbour, which Chichester itself is not, so stores could be conveniently landed here. Before long was added a modest house with a large colonnaded garden, which may well have been occupied by Cogidubnus. Then the house grew bigger. To the middle of the second century belongs the splendid floor, easily the finest of its type in Britain. It is like a sumptuous carpet, but in stone mosaic, with a boy on a dolphin in the centre (40).[1] But about 275 this palatial establishment was destroyed by fire, and never rebuilt.

Still more recently, fragments of another Roman mosaic floor have been found several feet below the south choir aisle of Chichester Cathedral. But in the town the principal legacies from the Romans are the plan and the line of the walls. They found an open settlement, and so for a long time it remained. Characteristically, one of their first acts was to regularise the plan. They made two straight streets through the town, one running north-south and the other east-west, and intersecting at the centre. This plan has never been changed. At Chichester, the Roman cross plan, first evolved about nineteen hundred years ago, is still the one (1, 2, 39).[2]

The *pax romana* was so effective in this part of Britain that it was not until the closing years of the second century that the town's first walls went up, and they were only modest earth ramparts, protected by an outer ditch. A little later flints, heavily mortared, were introduced as an external facing material. If stone was wanted in Chichester without the expense of importing it from elsewhere, it just had to be flint. There was nothing else.

[1] The figures in brackets refer to the plate numbers.

[2] The north-south street is slightly staggered at the centre, and it seems possible that this (not unattractive) misalignment is also Roman. The late Dr Francis Steer has suggested that it may be due to the existence of a Forum on the site now mainly occupied by the Dolphin and Anchor Hotel.

3. *A section of the city walls*

Flint, however, which is always associated with chalk, was available in unlimited quantities on the nearby South Downs. Scattered about on the land wherever the soil had been turned over, it needed nothing but to be gathered and transported. No other people has ever made as much use of it as we have. In the southern and eastern counties, starting with the Romans, it was for centuries a great standby.

After the walls came the bastions, probably sixteen of them in all. The area enclosed was not a rectangle but an eleven-sided polygon. It still is. But the walls which we see here today are not Roman. England has four towns where the walls are still fairly complete, and all four have a Roman inheritance. At York and Chester the walled area was enlarged in the Middle Ages. Here, as at Colchester, it was not: the walls and bastions, although medieval, follow the line of their Roman predecessors exactly (3).

Moreover, at Chichester we can still walk along considerable stretches. In the eighteenth century, when the streets were still unpaved, to walk along the top of the walls was often the most agreeable way of getting from one part of the town to another. But the four gates, first erected by the Romans, were all removed during the reign of George III: three of them in 1772 and the last, the East gate, eleven years later.

Until recently it was believed that the Romans kept the name of the town's first settlers, and called it Regnum. In 1957, however, in his monograph *Chichester as the Romans called it*, Judge Edward Done argued very convincingly that in fact the correct name was Noviomagus Regensium. This did not long survive the occupation of the town in 477 by the Saxons, who probably made their earliest landing in England between Selsey and East Wittering, about eight miles to the south-west. The first Saxon invader had a son called Cissa, and the place, according to tradition at any rate, became Cissa's *ceaster* (camp), from which derives the name Chichester. And that is just about all that this town owes to the Saxons.

Very different is its debt to the Normans, for it was they who built the Cathedral. Not the spire, and not the detached belfry, but most of the rest. The episcopal see, established first at Selsey in 681, was moved here by the Council of London, presided over by Archbishop Lanfranc, in 1075.

By Norman standards this is not by any means a spectacular church. It is evident that in this diocese money was short. The progress of building was slow: it lasted almost a hundred years. Nor was the quality of the original building very good. Flint, the only local stone, was clearly (and rightly) regarded as too humble for a cathedral. So the walls, outside and in, are of limestone. But it is only a facing.

There are in fact several kinds of limestone here, and they differ considerably. The first one to be used was Quarr stone brought over from the Isle of Wight. This is a hard Tertiary limestone which on the whole has worn very well. It has a most distinctive appearance, produced by tiny shell fragments deposited in fresh water. In some places it looks rather like a bed of feathers. But in 1187, only three years after the consecration, there was a very bad fire, and for the rebuilding they used quite a different sort of limestone which came from Caen in Normandy, just across the Channel. This is a Jurassic stone, and quite a good one too, with a much finer consistency than the other; but after nearly eight hundred years some of the blocks have flaked and spalled rather

4. The Cathedral from the garden of the Bishop's Palace

badly. On the south side of the nave it is instructive to see these two stones juxtaposed in the same wall.

Far and away the most notable feature of the pre-fire building is the pair of reliefs which were originally part of a screen or perhaps a reredos. They date from about 1140 and are now built into the wall of the south choir aisle. They were clearly inspired by an illuminated manuscript, which was almost certainly the St Albans Psalter, long a treasure of St Godehard's church at Hildesheim, near Hanover. In the first scene (5) Christ, attended by three (and formerly four) disciples, is just arriving at the house of Mary and Martha at Bethany. The two women, grief-stricken over the death of their

5. *Christ at the house of Mary and Martha*

6. *The raising of Lazarus*

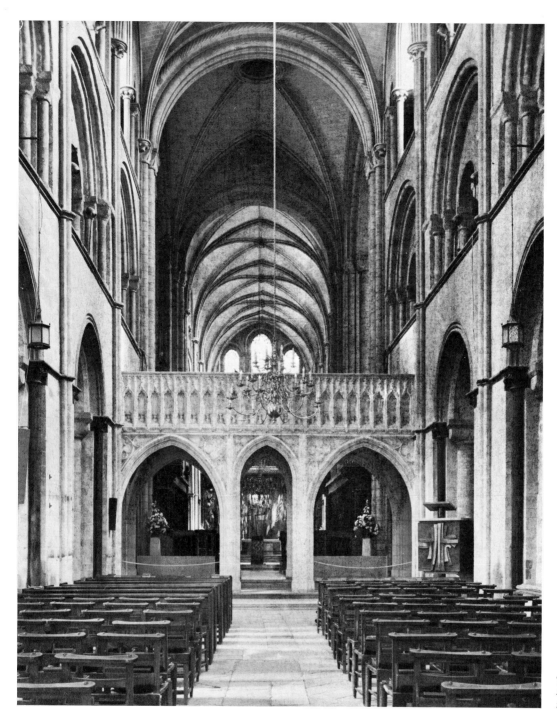

7. *The Arundel screen from the west*

brother, are pleading for his help. Strong and determined, Christ seems engrossed in thought. In the second scene (6) the miracle has been performed. Only Lazarus and the pair of old grave-diggers are passive; for the latter this was just another job of work. Christ, again represented as larger than the other figures, is a creation of the most tender humanity. Unforgettable are the faces of Mary and Martha, overwhelmed now with tears of gratitude. The disappearance of the coloured paste which is believed to have filled the eyes of all these people is a positive asset. These are certainly among the most precious Romanesque sculptures in England.

Architecturally the most satisfying part of the Cathedral's interior is the retrochoir, which is stylistically a bridge between the Norman and the earliest Gothic. This belongs to the phase of rebuilding that followed the fire. The piers and their surrounding shafts introduce yet another limestone, brought from the Purbeck peninsula in Dorset, and, like the others, by water, the only way of moving bulky materials any distance in the Middle Ages. This stone is usually referred to as Purbeck marble, because it will take a polish and retain it very well inside, though not outside a building. But the name is misleading, for this is not a marble but a shelly limestone, much in demand in England during the closing years of the twelfth century and throughout the thirteenth. From the long shallow beds slender monolithic shafts could be obtained, and these at Chichester are of quite exceptional size (8, 9).

The fifteenth-century pulpitum, known as the Arundel screen, was removed in 1860 – very fortunately as it turned out – and replaced in 1961 (7). It is a handsome piece, but personally I would not have put it back: the cathedral is relatively so small that the obstruction seems uncalled for, far superior as it is to the wooden screen of 1889 by Bodley and Garner, which was removed to make room for it. Through it can be seen the new reredos, installed in 1966, which takes the form of a tapestry designed by John Piper and woven at Aubusson in France.

8, 9.
In the retrochoir

The elegant stone spire was originally completed about 1400. The tower that carried it was very badly built. At the time they were not only short of money but of stone too. Although faced with blocks of freestone six to eight inches thick outside and in, the infilling was just a hodge-podge of chalk from the Downs mixed with flints, flinty pebbles from the sea-shore, and a lot of mortar. The facing, as so often in the Norman period, was not well bonded into the core. When the Arundel screen was removed, alarming cracks and fissures were revealed. Thereafter the drama quickly gathered momentum. In January 1861 adjacent walls started bulging. On 16 February an attempt was begun to encase the two worst affected piers in baulks of timber, hooped together with iron bolts. Four nights later, as a violent storm blew, the spire rocked and swayed. By noon on 21 February it became clear that nothing could save it. Seventy men were brought down just in time. At exactly half past one the spire descended perpendicularly into the church, and much of the tower came with it. No one was even injured.

The rebuilding was very well done by Sir George Gilbert Scott. For once he did not try to improve upon the original (4). But the stone he used was Tisbury, a sandy oolitic limestone from Wiltshire, and it has worn none too well. This of course is a very exposed position, which presents a severe test for any stone, but there are now pockets of decay several inches deep. So the Cathedral is having to undergo further extensive and prolonged restoration. For the new stone the Dean and Chapter have turned once again to France: Courteraie limestone from the Meuse *Département* is the one now principally employed.

At 277 feet this excellent spire (incidentally, the only English cathedral spire to be visible from the sea) is of course the focal point of the whole design (2, 4), for the squat western towers in no way compete. Nor, fortunately, does the detached bell-tower, built early in the fifteenth century to relieve the central tower of the strain of bell-ringing – fears must have been felt for it, even as early as this. The bell-tower, although rather a dull design, is of interest as being the one medieval building in Chichester which is of sandstone. The stone is Green Ventnor, from the greensand beds of the Isle of Wight. Its surface is badly decayed.

Chichester Cathedral is very much part of its city. There is not even a railing now between West Street and the Close, which is exactly as it should be. At the south-western corner of the Close is the early Gothic chapel of the Bishop's Palace. This is a beautiful stone-vaulted building which harbours the little wall-painting known as the Chichester Roundel, executed about 1250 (10). The subject is the Virgin and Child, with censing angels. It is sad that the silver used for the censers has oxidised and turned black, for nothing can be done about this. The rose-pink is also much faded. But the blue, which is lapis-lazuli, is fairly well preserved, and so is the gold, employed for the crown, the child's halo, the head of the sceptre, the handles of the swinging censers and the *fleurs-de-lis* powdered over the blue ground. This is not only one of our loveliest early Gothic wall-paintings but also, despite the darkening of the silver, one of the best

preserved. The mood is gentle and tender; the composition singularly harmonious.

A few yards away, across the passage, is the former kitchen, with rough walls of whitewashed flint and a strictly functional timber roof (11) which until early in the present century had a central flue open to the sky. But to see a much grander example of medieval carpentry we can go to St Mary's Hospital, erected as an almshouse just before 1300. The roof here (12), remarkably well preserved, has none of the refinement nor decorative enrichment to be achieved a century later in Westminster Hall and two centuries later in many Perpendicular wool churches, especially in East Anglia; but this, it must be remembered, is nearly seven hundred years old. Basically it is a trussed-rafter roof, which sweeps down to within seven feet of the ground. But such weight, needless to say, required additional support. This was provided by the insertion, at intervals, of big oak tie-beams carried on enormous oak posts, to which the weight is transferred by two sets of braces on each side. From the centre of each tie-beam a crown-post rises to a short horizontal beam called a collar. It is all a bit clumsy – barn-like, in fact – but structurally it works, admirably; and incidentally it illustrates the use of yet another local material, oak, which was so abundant in this county as to be known in the Middle Ages as 'the Sussex weed'.

11 *(far left).*
Old kitchen of the Bishop's Palace

12 *(left).*
St Mary's Hospital

St Mary's Hospital has always been an almshouse, but architecturally it resembles a church in having a 'nave' and a 'chancel'. The nave now has four bays; originally there were two more to the west. What is remarkable is that, unlike any other building of its kind in England, it is still lived in. Under the enormous roof there are seven tiny, self-contained sets of rooms: self-contained, that is, except for a bathroom, which was installed in what used to be the eighth set. At the east end, in what I have compared to the chancel of a church, is the chapel, approached through a fine screen, also of about 1300. The chapel is memorable for its misericords, which are superior to those in the Cathedral. Deservedly famous is the Merman (14). How the carver relished the oakiness of his oak!

The low walls of the Hospital are built of flint, with minimal stone dressings, and this was the material which, twenty years earlier, the Grey Friars had also used for their church. Or rather for the choir of their church, for it seems that the nave was never built. The choir still stands, in Priory Park – a striking fragment, converted in 1541 into the City Guildhall (13). It is now part of the City Museum.

13. *Greyfriars, once the church of the Franciscans*

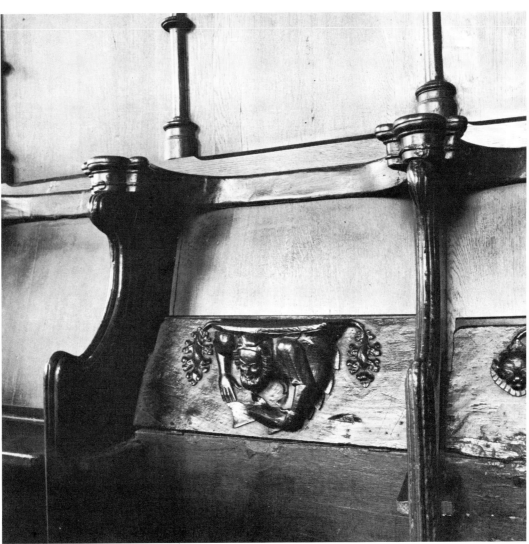

14. *The Merman misericord, St Mary's Hospital chapel*

But in 1501, for the Market Cross (16), they went back to Caen stone. This was a present to the city – and what a present! – from one of the bishops, Edward Story, whose tomb is in the Cathedral. Unhappily, it suffered in the Civil War. The rather inappropriate cupola dates only from 1746; the clock was given in 1724. But, situated as it is at the point where the four principal streets meet – or, if you prefer, where the two Roman streets intersect – the Market Cross is a delightful feature of many Chichester views.

For churches, but not for much else, the limestone tradition continued. St Peter, West Street, by R. C. Carpenter, best known as the architect of Lancing College Chapel, is unusually pleasing for its date (begun in 1848). The masoncraft is of high quality, and so is some of the carved detail on the west porch, an addition of 1881. But it is a church no more.

15. *24 South Street*

On the domestic side the picture is quite different. Until the closing years of the seventeenth century, in Chichester as in so many other English towns, most of the houses were timber-framed. A certain number of these framed houses still stand, and here and there, under the much later rendering, a jetty – that is, an overhanging upper storey – leaves no room for doubt about the underlying structure (15). But almost all the timber-framed houses which were not demolished were refronted in the eighteenth century, so externally wood plays next to no part today in the Chichester scene.

The rebuilding of the town in brick began shortly before 1700, and the array of fine surviving Georgian houses is evidence that it persisted throughout the eighteenth century. Daniel Defoe, writing in the 1720s, remarked that 'the city is not a place of much trade, nor is it very populous'. Nevertheless, as an American once said to me about

16. *The Market Cross*

Baltimore, there must have been a lot of quiet money here. The corn trade flourished, and so did the general market, while only a mile away there was the port.

The earliest important domestic building in brick is still one of the most stately: the John Edes House in West Street (17). (From 1841 until 1905 this was known as Westgate House, and in the Sussex *Buildings of England* volume this is still its name. In 1905 it became West Street House, and in 1911, quite unhistorically, Wren House. In 1967 the name was changed again, and, much more appropriately, it is now called after the man who built it. Today it houses the County and Diocesan Record offices.) Dating from 1696, it is, with its mullioned and transomed casement windows in Portland stone, its slightly projecting wings and its strong eaves-cornice in white-painted wood, a very typical building of the later Stuart period.

17. *The John Edes House*

What unhappily is also all too typical of this country is that this house, with the most imposing front in Chichester, should be condemned to hide behind two enormous magnolia trees. They do not even flower very well on this cramped site, but the very idea of cutting them down would be, I do not doubt, to some people deeply shocking. Nevertheless it should be done, and preferably tomorrow. I yield to no one in my pleasure in flowering magnolias in the right place, but that is definitely not here.

Sixteen years later came another of the town's outstanding brick buildings: Pallant House, built by Henry Peckham, a prosperous wine merchant, in 1712 (18). He was evidently determined to build regardless of expense, so he was fortunate in having at his disposal craftsmen who could help him to fulfil his ambitions. Each of the window-

18. *Pallant House (now furnished and containing Dean Walter Hussey's art collection, open Tuesday to Saturday, 10.00 to 5.30)*

heads has bricks specially gauged, and every key-block has a carved emblem, rose, thistle, *fleur-de-lis* or harp, while the base of each one is cut back in delicately recessed curves. The parapet displays still greater virtuosity. Above each window a sunk panel, the upper edge of which appears to have been 'gathered' like the soft pelmet of a curtain (21). Imagine cutting this in brick!

Nor is this a grand house on a country estate: it was just a merchant's house in a prosperous market town. That these middle-class people were now both able and willing to pay for the choicest refinements – although the gates have gone, another is the wrought-iron overthrow between the gate-piers (20), an exquisite piece of blacksmith's craftsmanship – is one of the factors which make small towns rich in Queen Anne and Georgian architecture, like Chichester, one of England's greatest delights. Within, it is not at all surprising to find a beautiful staircase (19). On the landing there is another Corinthian doorcase which was obviously the work of the same joiner as the one facing the street.

Pallant House is surrounded on every side by Georgian houses of high quality, all admirably maintained. Chichester's four main streets divide the town into what, for convenience, are called quadrants (40). That to the north-west was still largely unbuilt

19. *Pallant House, staircase*

20. *Pallant House, entrance*

21. *Pallant House, a window*

on in the eighteenth century, and holds little of interest. The south-west quadrant contains the Cathedral and, apart from the Deanery of 1725, an exceptionally unengaging house for its date, not much that is Georgian. The best houses of this period are all to be found either in the four main streets themselves, and especially North Street, or in the north-east or south-east quadrants. The latter is the best and most unspoiled of all, and the four Pallants, themselves arranged in the form of a cross, echo in miniature the plan of the town itself. It is at Pallant House that these four short streets meet. All four contain eighteenth-century brick houses of real distinction: 3–5 East Pallant (22), 1 North Pallant (23) and 12 West Pallant (24), illustrated here, are but three examples.

Sussex, and indeed the whole of the South-East, is a part of England renowned for the quality of its brickwork. This was no doubt partly dependent upon the skill of the local brickmakers in a region where, by 1700, there was already a long tradition of brick manufacture. It was also due to the good fortune of the South-East in possessing exactly the right clays. Two kinds of clay were needed for the best bricks, the one plastic, the other sandy. In the eighteenth century the two were blended in what was known as a pug-mill, from which emerged a smooth dough, with all the pebbles and other impurities removed. But in the kiln the bricks were not all burnt equally. Some were fired more than others, and those with the most heavily burnt ends would emerge darker, and sometimes, according to the chemical composition of the clay, semi-vitrified (or glazed). This variation in colour and tone is aesthetically very important.

22. 3–5 East Pallant

23 *(right).*
1 North Pallant

24 *(far right).*
2 West Pallant

25. *2 East Row*

26. *11–14 St John's Street*

27 *(right).*
6 and 7 Cavendish Street

28 *(far right).*
5 North Pallant

A little early Georgian house in East Row (25) provides a perfect illustration. This house was old-fashioned in still being built with English bond: that is, with one row of stretchers (bricks laid sideways) and one of headers (bricks laid end on) alternating. That had given place to Flemish bond (alternating headers and stretchers in the same course) nearly everywhere in England by 1700. But the quality of the brickwork is lovely. The warm vermilions so characteristic of these Sussex bricks were due to the presence of iron in the clay.

Now and again, however, a chalkier clay was used, with enough lime in it to counteract the particles of iron. This yielded the so-called 'white' bricks (actually pale yellow), which were considered smarter than red in the first half of the nineteenth century, presumably because they looked more like stone. There can be no doubt about this, for at 14 St John's Street (26) the side elevation is red, the front 'white'. These 'white' bricks are certainly the acme of refinement.

Elsewhere the burnt headers, in varying shades of grey, were used to make patterns. This was a practice which went right back to the Tudor period, when diamond-shaped diapers were much enjoyed. In the Georgian age a uniform colour was generally preferred; when it was decided to have a diaper, it was always an all-over chequer pattern: red stretchers and grey headers.

These grey headers were so much esteemed that here and there they were used to face an entire front. Cavendish Street has a number of good examples (27). Against their subdued colour the bright red rubbed bricks over the windows shine out with special brilliance. But most of Chichester's Georgian houses are red and only red, and who

29 *(right).*
3 St Martin's Square

30. *43 North Street*

could want it otherwise? 8 St Martin's Square (31) provides a charming variation, in that almost all the facing bricks are headers.

Where there are good bricks, there are usually good tiles too, and this is certainly true of Chichester, where some of the roofscapes are rich in both colour and texture. There are no old pantiles, those S-section roof tiles which were first imported into this country from Holland at the beginning of the eighteenth century. In this part of England the

31. 8 St Martin's Square

tiles are plain, with average dimensions about ten inches by six, and half an inch thick. But these handmade, sand-faced tiles endow any building that has them with a marvellous sense of quality (29, 30).

Surprisingly, however, there are very few hung tiles in Chichester: surprisingly, because south-eastern England is where tile-hanging appeared first and where there is far more of it than anywhere else. It served, especially on timber-framed houses, to give protection against the weather, but no doubt its appeal was also aesthetic – as it still is.

Unceasing sources of pleasure in Chichester are the Georgian doorcases and the fanlights over the doors, which show considerable variation (28, 32–35). Sometimes it is just the doorcase, or just the fanlight that strikes the attention, but often it is both. The owners are evidently proud of them, as they have every reason to be, for almost all of them are impeccably maintained.

The quality of the brickwork here is so good that it comes as something of a surprise to discover how often it has been covered with some sort of rendering. A number of these houses have trowel-lines incised on the stucco to suggest stone blocks: that was a very common practice in south-eastern England in the first part of the nineteenth century. Where that occurs, the surfacing is of course always stone-coloured, but elsewhere, more recently, other colours have been introduced. Although my instinct would be to hold that, with brickwork as good as Chichester's, it is rather a pity to hide it under any kind of rendering, it has to be acknowledged that those pleasantly varied colours do add a note of liveliness to some of the streets.

Stone was hardly used for house-building in Chichester before 1800. Then flint made quite an impressive reappearance. 40 North Street (36) is a stately Regency house probably built about 1820. With its gracious Tuscan Doric porch, its large sash-framed windows with their elegant glazing bars, and its broad eaves, this house is wholly characteristic of its time. But it has one remarkable feature – its flints, employed in a far more sophisticated way than by the Romans or in the Middle Ages.

The origin of flint is obscure. Geologically it is a silica, and exceedingly hard: indeed, virtually indestructible. Through contact with chalk, it usually develops a kind of white 'rind' over the entire surface. But, although so hard, flints can be split open quite easily by anyone who knows how to do it, and when they have been fractured they are found to be shiny and often nearly black inside. The fracturing process is known as knapping. Nearly all the flints on the front of 40 North Street were knapped, and also laid in courses, with dressings in pale yellow brick; and very good they look.

Nevertheless, every flint wall has an Achilles heel, which is the mortar. The shapes of flint nodules are sometimes so amorphous that, even when knapped, a great deal of mortar is required. And it is always the mortar which decays first. Then the flints may easily fall out. To mask the big area of mortar, and perhaps also to strengthen it, recourse was had to a curious technique known as galleting. This involved the prepara-

36. *40 North Street*

tion of slivers of flint and pressing them into the mortar while it was still wet. Never was galleting used with greater profusion than at Chichester. 40 North Street is a remarkable but by no means unique example of it.

Another instance, also from the Regency period, is 44 South Street (37). Here there is not so much knapping, but the coursing is more regular: this was achieved by selecting flints of about the same size. A way of realising this effect without knapping was to gather smooth, water-washed flint pebbles from some nearby beach; and Chichester also has examples of this.

The observant visitor will not fail to notice that the fascia boards of the Chichester shops are well above the usual standard (30, 38). This is no accident. Strict control is exercised: every shop has to obtain planning permission for its board. Needless to say, there is no thought of uniformity. Apart from a good standard of lettering, what matters is

37. 44 South Street

38. *74–78 North Street*

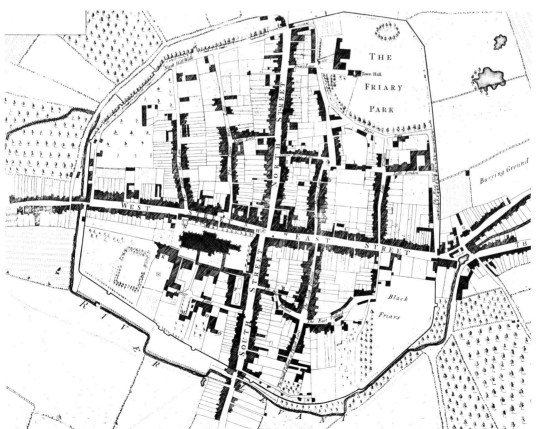

39. *William Gardner's plan of the city, 1769*

the scale of the fasciae, both in relation to each other and to the buildings of which they are a part. Would that every town would take a leaf out of Chichester's book. The powers exist, but it would seem that all too often the local Council just does not bother. It should.

Illuminated signs are also very unwelcome here. And so are stickers on shop windows, one of the special eyesores of the present day. They are not allowed here, except for short periods during sales. As somebody said not long ago, shopkeepers would do better to display their wares than their words.

In recent years Chichester has gained the admiration of all who cherish historic towns by showing a greater concern for pedestrians than, I believe, any other town in England. The ancient plan, as indicated earlier, has been preserved here with unusual completeness. Except in the north-western quadrant, where the County Council's offices now loom too large, there is not really a great deal of difference, inside the walls, between the plan which William Gardner made in 1769 and what is to be found today. (Outside is another matter, but the motor traffic has to go somewhere.) The inner portions of North Street and East Street have been entirely closed after 9 am to wheeled traffic, which in South and West Streets has been severely restricted. For parking cars inside the walls one pays, whereas outside it is free.

Pedestrianisation was not decided upon without a very thorough enquiry, with traffic surveys and extremely comprehensive public consultation. As was only to be expected, there were objectors; but approximately two out of every three of the local people were in favour of it, including the large majority of shoppers, particularly those with children, and almost everybody concerned with the well-being of the urban environment. As for non-resident visitors, nearly all are delighted. The streets are not wide enough for planting, but a few seats should now be introduced. One point that has emerged, here as elsewhere, is that most of the shops do not really suffer from the pedestrian precinct; in fact, some shops on the 'walking streets' are, on balance, probably better off. That was something which Copenhagen discovered many years ago.

Chichester has a by-pass which takes most of the heavy traffic; there is also an inner-ring road which, on the south-west side, has wrought havoc with Westgate Fields, once an area of quiet recreation with delightful Cathedral views. Yet, compared with what has happened in recent years in many other places, Chichester has come off lightly.

With the population now approaching 25,000, this is not only the oldest but the largest of the six towns in my collection. But this figure includes the new housing estates on the periphery. For the visitor, and for the amateur of architecture in particular, almost all the interest is concentrated within an area of not much more than a hundred acres, delineated by the ancient walls. Small and compact, it is an almost perfect place in which to live and work. 'Chichester', wrote the late Dr Thomas Sharp in 1949, 'is a very special city indeed . . . which probably holds more of the purity and true essence of its type than any now remaining in England. It is an important and irreplaceable part of the national heritage.'

40. *Fishbourne's finest floor*

RICHMOND

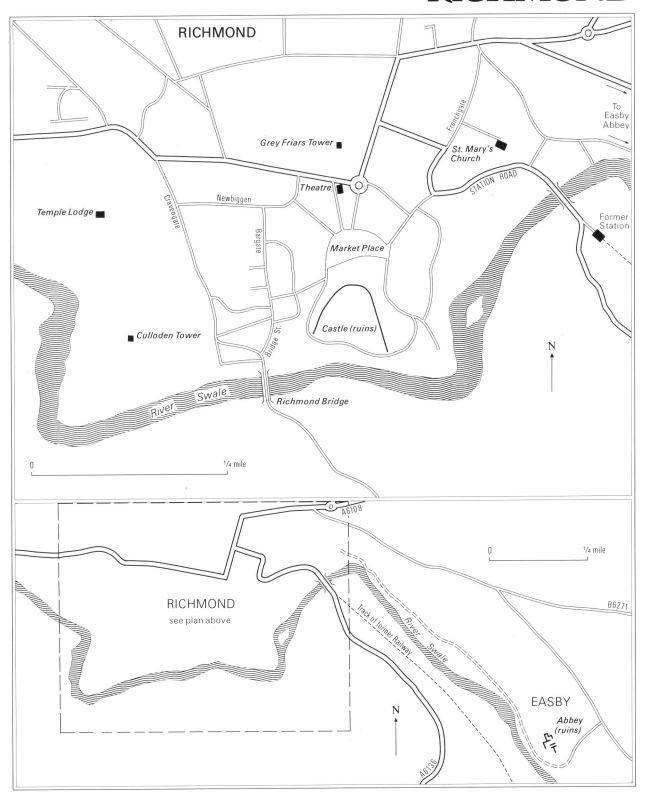

RICHMOND

Grey Friars Tower

St. Mary's Church

Frenchgate

Theatre

STATION ROAD

To Easby Abbey

Former Station

Temple Lodge

Cravengate

Newbiggen

Bargate

Market Place

Culloden Tower

Bridge St.

Castle (ruins)

N

River Swale

Richmond Bridge

0   ¼ mile

A6108

0   ¼ mile

RICHMOND
see plan above

Track of former Railway

River Swale

B6271

N

A6136

EASBY

Abbey (ruins)

1. *Richmond – town plan*

'From Darlington it was ten miles, and very tedious miles. . . . Richmond town one cannot see till just upon it, being encompass'd with great high hills. I descended a very steep hill to it from whence saw the whole town which itself stands on a hill tho' not so high as those by it. There is a very large space for the Markets which are divided for the fish market flesh market and corn; there is a large Market Crosse and by it a Church and the ruines of a Castle. The buildings are all stone and the streetes are like rocks themselves.'

So wrote that intrepid horsewoman Celia Fiennes in her diary nearly three hundred years ago, and how right she was! Although nearly all relaid in concrete now to take today's heavy vehicles, most of the older streets of Richmond are still cobbled. They do not make for smooth walking, but picturesque they surely are, and the local people are devoted to them. Freely gathered from the bed of the river Swale, they are certainly one of the most characteristic features of this small, ancient North Yorkshire town (3, 29).

Richmond originated with the Normans. The very name, *Riche-mont* ('strong hill'), is French in origin. It was in 1068 that the Conqueror, after a successful battle at York, bestowed upon his second cousin, Alan Rufus of Brittany, who had come over with him, the princely domain of the former Saxon Earl of Mercia (who in Yorkshire alone had owned 199 manors). It was either Alan or more probably his son who was created 1st

3. *Cobbles in Bargate*

4. The Castle from the south

Earl of Richmond: Alan died in 1089 and the name does not occur until 1090. Even so, that was nearly four centuries before there was a Richmond in Surrey. It was only when the earldom passed to the first Tudor monarch, Henry VII, that the name of the Yorkshire town was also given to the royal palace at Sheen.

Alan built his castle here not so much to protect England from the Scots as to protect himself from the local Anglo-Saxons. It was a magnificent site, accessible only from one side, the north. So this is where the gatehouse was, and it was on top of the gatehouse that, in the third quarter of the twelfth century, was erected the still very imposing sandstone Keep (2). The Great Court is roughly triangular, and at least on the east side the original curtain wall of the late eleventh century survives intact, notable for the incorporation of sections of herring-bone masonry, best seen from the smaller enclosure known as the Cockpit.

Close to the Cockpit is the Great Hall, or Scolland's Hall as it is called here: he was the sewer (hall superintendent) to the first Earl. It is one of the earliest large castle halls in the country, and perhaps the first of any, having also been completed before the end of the eleventh century. Sited on the edge of a precipice, the views from below and from the hill facing it across the Swale are sensational (4).

It was one of the Constables of the Castle who in 1155 founded, a mile downstream, the Abbey of St Agatha at Easby. This was for Premonstratensian canons, a strict order who, like the Cistercians, wore a white habit, so were generally known as the White Canons, as distinct from the ordinary Augustinian or Black Canons.

Of the church itself not much survives, but the frater, or refectory, on the south side of the cloister is still impressive. Most of the stone at Easby is very rubbly; for the in-filling of the walls the monks principally relied on cobbles from the river Swale. But the frater, standing over a vaulted undercroft, was largely rebuilt about 1300, and the wall was then faced externally with well-dressed sandstone, which was also used for the window tracery. There were five noble windows, very large, on the side away from the cloister, and a broad five-light east window with much of its tracery still intact (6).

Also ruinous but in a fair state of preservation is the front of the solar or upstairs living-room, part of the *hospitium*, added early in the thirteenth century for the accommodation of guests (5). Another survival is the gatehouse, also of about 1300. This has been well restored; the roofless upstairs room has a pair of two-light windows, again with Decorated tracery.

Richmond itself never had a major church. The town came into existence to serve the Castle. It was of course walled – and one of the gates, Cornforth Bar, survives (7) – but the area enclosed was very small: little, in fact, save the houses in the Market Place and the gardens that lay behind them. Only one church, Holy Trinity, lay within the walls: this was never the parish church and is now the Regimental Museum of the Green Howards. The parish church, St Mary, was always outside the walls (and well below the

5. *Easby Abbey guest-house from the south-east*

6. *Easby Abbey refectory, looking east*

7. *Cornforth Bar, Richmond*

8. *Grey Friars tower*

level of the castle), which was unusual. Perhaps the explanation is that the constricted area of the town on the hill did not allow sufficient space for a burial ground. The church was unhappily much marred in 1860.

When the Grey Friars (Franciscans) arrived in 1258, they too had to settle for an extramural site. Only the sandstone tower of their church remains, but, apart from the Castle, this is the only notable survivor of medieval Richmond. It was a central tower, oblong in plan, and dates only from the fifteenth century. Although modest compared with some of the great Yorkshire towers of the Perpendicular period of Gothic architecture, it is a considerable ornament to the town (8).

At the time that the Grey Friars tower went up, medieval Richmond had reached the zenith of its prosperity. It had been a market town from as far back as 1155, only ten years after it had obtained its first charter in return for an annual rent to the feudal lord, the Earl of Richmond. It was a general market, for corn, butter, cheese, fish, wine and salt: also for wool, hides, leather goods, timber, iron, lead and copper.

The houses were mostly timber-framed, but not a single one survives. By 1450 the population was about two thousand, and it did not exceed that figure until the Georgian period three hundred years later. John Speed's pictorial plan (9) shows that in 1610, when much more of the Castle was standing than today, and all three town gates, the houses were concentrated into about half a dozen streets, mostly steep. The irregularity of the plan was directly due to the hilliness of the site, which of course adds greatly to the town's picturesqueness.

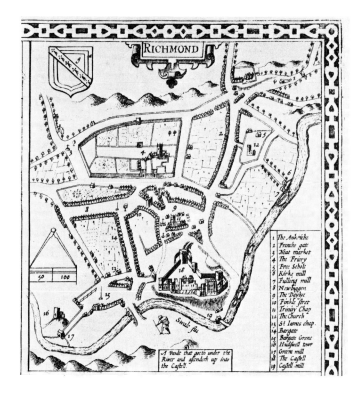

9. *John Speed's plan, 1610*

10 *(right).*
Valmont Lodge,
Bridge Street

11 *(far right).*
Minden House,
32 Frenchgate

By Speed's time a good many of the timber-framed houses had been rebuilt with rubblestone or cobbles, but even from the seventeenth century very little remains: about twenty houses in all, most of them considerably restored and much altered. The place was not prosperous: indeed, Celia Fiennes describes it as 'disregarded', and 'a sad shatter'd town fallen much to decay'. By now markets had opened in other North Yorkshire towns, so that Richmond's declined in importance. What saved it, as so often in England, was wool. After 1500, the people kept themselves alive chiefly by knitting. They knitted woollen stockings and caps, particularly for sailors. For nearly three centuries, everyone here knitted.

After about 1700, matters improved. The establishment of a modest clothing industry was followed by the starting of paper mills, and in the Victorian period there was considerable traffic in lead from the mines of the Pennines, as well as the corn market which now flourished.

Architecturally the old town is predominantly Georgian, and very largely built of stone. But there can be few towns in England in which the accurate identification of the stonework presents more problems. The reason is that there are at least four kinds of stone employed here for building, and not infrequently a single wall will contain a mixture. Two generalisations can be made with confidence: all Richmond's stone was obtained locally, and all of it is of great antiquity. Since it all belongs to the Carboniferous system, it must be over 300 million years old.

Less than a mile from the Market Place, towards the north-west, there were two limestone quarries. Both are now worked out and in process of being filled in, but both were still in use well within the present century. It is a very hard stone, but it could be quarried with hammers, iron bars and wedges without recourse to blasting. The colours are an amalgam of greys and pale browns. A smooth, ashlared finish was impossible; it is much too hard for that. But the rough texture looks very well here: Minden House, Frenchgate, built in 1759 (11), is typical.

There are worked-out quarries of Carboniferous sandstone, too, within carting distance of the town. One of the best, also largely filled with rubbish now, is on Gatherley Moor, four and a half miles away to the north. Where a freestone was required, they had to use sandstone. This is hard too, but not as hard as the limestone: it can be sawn if required. But although this pale, sandy brown stone was the favourite in Georgian Richmond, it was not usually ashlared. There was not much call for a smooth finish here, at least until the Victorian period, nor does the character of the town require it, as a house like Valmont Lodge (10), at the foot of Bridge Street, makes clear.

An excellent example of Gatherley Moor sandstone is Richmond Bridge. The story is extraordinary. The old bridge over the Swale was destroyed by a flood in 1771, but the northern half belonged to the Corporation and the southern half to the County. This led to years of bickering, even after they had agreed that John Carr of York should be the architect of the new bridge. There were separate contracts and separate contractors, and it is said that the County's half was finished three years before the Town's – although how one halves a three-arched stone bridge baffles me, I must confess! It is a very handsome structure (13), and shows that this sandstone could be obtained in substantial blocks, which the local limestone could not.

12. *The River Swale at Richmond*

13. Richmond Bridge

Much of Richmond's stone, however, did not require any quarrying; it only had to be lifted from the bed of the Swale. Not that this was always easy, for the Swale is known as the second swiftest river in England, and some of the hunks of stone carried down from the Pennine hills in periods of spate were very large. But there can be no doubt that an appreciable quantity of the town's sandstone masonry was drawn from the river (12). Also from the river-bed came an endless supply of cobbles, again mostly hard sandstone. These were always fragments of a parent rock, broken off by water or glacial ice and becoming more or less rounded in the course of their water-borne journey. The smaller ones were in demand for paving the streets; the bigger ones often went into walls. Some of the cottages near the river are constructed almost entirely of cobbles (14). In other buildings cobbles, usually brown, will be found interspersed with sandstone or limestone, or both, in rubblestone walls. And, although it is seldom possible to see them, because of course they are covered, I am assured that many of the internal walls of Richmond's older buildings are also built almost wholly of cobbles, laid, needless to say, in plenty of mortar. This is in fact yet one more example of pre-Industrial Revolution builders making use of whatever material was most conveniently accessible.

To the south-west, between Richmond and Leyburn, the stone becomes what is known locally as 'bastard': that is, a stone in which the ingredients are mixed – the progeny, it might be said, of a limestone father and a sandstone mother. Such mixtures occur in other geological systems, too: there are, for example, Cretaceous and Jurassic

14. *Castle Terrace*

limestones which are decidedly sandy, and sandstones, such as Reigate, that are markedly calcareous. Although not much used in Richmond itself, this 'bastard' stone can often be seen at farmhouses and their outbuildings a little way up the Dale.

Yet another stone to be found here, curious and not very well known, is chert. In character this is comparable with flint: a kind of silica and intensely hard, occurring in lumpy nodules, or sometimes even in narrow beds of its own, in the Carboniferous limestone. (Elsewhere, chert occurs in other rocks too: in east Devon and south-west Somerset, for instance, in the Upper Greensand. Considerable use was made of it for building in that area.) At Richmond whole walls of chert are unusual, although one house, 15 Bridge Street (15), appears to be mainly built of it; but many Richmond buildings display lumps of chert incorporated into walls of limestone rubble. It is nevertheless quite understandable that people should usually have preferred to build with stone that was rather less intractable.

It was the sandstone that supplied the 'slates', or flagstones as they are sometimes called in the North, for all the older roofs. A fair number of these survive, and their sombre splendour suits the locality to perfection. They vary considerably in size, and were always laid in graduated courses: the largest, at the base of the roof, might be as much as four feet by three, and two inches thick, and two strong men would be needed to lift them. The smallest, laid at the ridge, would be about twelve inches by nine, with a thickness of half an inch. Stone slates as massive as these demanded, needless to say,

15. *15 Bridge Street*

very strong support: rafters four inches broad and two inches thick were by no means rare. Even so, the sagging roof is a common – and, it should be added, by no means a displeasing – sight. But it was always the supporting framework which decayed first, and, whenever this occurred, there was a continuing temptation to replace it with something lighter, which could only carry Welsh slates or tiles (16). Nobody could hold that either of these agrees with Richmond's stone buildings so well. On brick buildings, of course, the tiles are perfectly appropriate.

The tiles here, as usual in the north-eastern towns, are not plain but pan. Pantiles did not appear in England until the eighteenth century. They are considerably larger than plain tiles, but in fact more economical, because in the downward direction they overlap only one, not two, courses below, and can be laid at a flatter pitch than plain tiles. Thus the pantiled roof is the lighter of the two, and can be supported on less robust roof-timbers. They are often very enjoyable. The rhythmical surging of the courses yields a most satisfying texture. Towards evening there is also a play of light and shade over the surface which is very pleasing. They are usually red, and a good deal more attractive than the bricks. Some were made locally, but it seems that the majority were brought from tileries elsewhere in the area. Some certainly came from Darlington, but the best pantiles within easy access were made at Boroughbridge.

Bricks were not used at Richmond before the eighteenth century, and even now are not very common in the historic parts of the town. From the Georgian period the only striking brick building is the King's Head in the Market Place (17, 29), and even here

16. *Richmond roofs in 1944*

17. *The King's Head*

the dressings (most of them unfortunately smothered with brown paint) are of stone. Nor, to be frank, is Richmond's brickwork very attractive. The reason is that they just did not have the best clays here, as they did in the South and East. These hard carbonaceous clays, as can be seen in many parts of the North, lack the plasticity of other and younger clays, nor do they fire to such agreeable hues: that is a matter of their chemical composition. But at least these are not the harsh reds of some parts of Lancashire and the Midlands.

Whether the houses are of brick or of stone, however, the architectural pleasures of Georgian Richmond tend to be centred on details rather than upon the ensemble. Although it cannot be said that the doorcases equal Chichester's, some, particularly in Frenchgate (18–20), are not without charm. (Incidentally Richmond, like other towns in the Eastern Midlands and North-East, especially Yorkshire, has a number of street names ending in 'gate'. The word is of Scandinavian origin: *gata* in old Norse meant a road or street, and the area of its currency roughly corresponds with that of the Danelaw.) But even from the Georgian period it has to be admitted that, architecturally, Richmond cannot show us a single outstanding house. The reason, no doubt, is that the town was never affluent.

A building here with rather a special character is the Theatre. This was opened in 1788, closed in the 1840s, and reopened in 1963. During the long interval it was floored at stage level and the whole pit was filled by a vaulted wine cellar. But fortunately the vaults were erected inside the original walls and were therefore removable. What has emerged since the restoration is the best preserved and without question the most authentic Georgian theatre in the country (21).

All the interest is within. The theatre has been redecorated in the original colours, mainly shades of green, based on one panel which was rediscovered after six coats of overpainting had been laboriously removed. The red for the canvas hangings lining the boxes also recalls the original scheme. On the lintels of both the doors leading from the front of the stage are painted swags with the masks of Comedy and Tragedy. The painted woodland scenery, on permanent loan from the Society of Theatrical Craftsmen and Designers, is the oldest in England: it dates from 1836. The stage is narrow but deep, so the perspective effect, enhanced by a raking floor, is excellent. Formerly there were three trap-doors too, with machinery, no doubt, to allow actors to rise on platforms and disappear into the depths.

The theatre seats 237 people, and it must be said that, for comfort, small, short people are at a considerable advantage. Nor can so minuscule a theatre stand on its own feet without financial help from outside. But it is good that Richmond should have this tiny living theatre because, as Ivor Brown observed, the little town 'is itself a piece of theatre, surging dramatically up from the gorge of the Swale to its castle, market and clustered, hillside homes'.

21. *The Georgian Theatre*

22. *Culloden Tower*

What is perhaps Richmond's most remarkable Georgian building is Georgian at its most uncharacteristic. Culloden Tower (22) was built in 1747 by a Mr Yorke to celebrate – and it was indeed, many will feel, a matter for celebration – the crushing, finally and for ever, of any hopes for the return to the throne of Britain of the House of Stuart. His son had fought in the battle. The tower is splendidly sited on a spot where, long before, there had been a pele-tower: that is to say, a keep standing in isolation, of which the existing rectangular base, in rubblestone, may well be a part. The two upper storeys, faced with smooth sandstone, are octagonal, and at one corner a projecting turret contains a spiral staircase crowned by a small domed cap. The view from the roof is a delight, with the river in a wooded valley just below and the Castle on its loftier hill to the East.

Within, there is one good room on each floor, and most of the ornamental details are Gothick, the term used for Georgian improvisation on the medieval style. On the first floor there is a most attractive chimney-piece, some pleasing woodwork and a pretty plaster vault. On the second floor the classical mode predominates and the decoration is less exuberant. Culloden Tower stands in isolation in private grounds, but has been taken over by the Landmark Trust, skilfully restored, and turned into a viable holiday residence.

A less ambitious but decidedly entertaining example of Richmond's Gothick is 47 Newbiggin (23), built a generation later than the Tower. The material is again sandstone. The two principal ground-floor rooms have bay windows with mullions in the form of

23. *47 Newbiggin*

clustered columns, cusped heads and ornamented spandrels. Internally these bays are prettily rib-vaulted.

Temple Lodge (26), in whose lovely park Culloden Tower stands, is also Gothick. It is believed to have been built by John Yorke in 1769, but about 1850 it was enlarged, and the castellations are certainly early Victorian. The effect is notably picturesque, nor is there any of that rather gimcrack-looking cement rendering which, in some parts of the country, buildings of this type are all too liable to exhibit. All here is good sandstone.

Temple Lodge is on the western fringe of the historic town. Close to the eastern fringe, a little more than half a mile away, is a Gothick doorway which would not look at all out of place at the Lodge. Its date is known. It belongs, though, not to a country house but to what, until it was closed about 1963, was Richmond's railway station (25). The railway reached here in 1848 by means of a short branch from the main line of the North Eastern between York and Darlington. The station was a very pleasant building by the Yorkshire architect G. T. Andrews. But what is so excellent is that in this case we can say not only 'was' but 'is'! For it was bought by the District Council, who have leased it as a Garden Centre (24).

This is a shining example of what enterprise and imagination can do to save a good building no longer required for its original purpose. All over the country there are still stations – well over a thousand of them, some well designed and perfectly capable of adaptation – which stand empty and a prey to vandals. So this is an object lesson for us

24, 25. *The old railway station*

26. *Temple Lodge*

all. Some of the most enjoyable buildings are, or were, stations, and it is sheer folly to destroy them or leave them to be vandalised when they might be transformed, as this one has been, and put to really good use. And across the road the former stationmaster's house is now the home of an architect.

To provide access to their station from the town, the Railway Company had to construct another bridge over the Swale, which continued the Gothick theme. This is now known as the Mercury Bridge, a reference to the regimental emblem of the Royal Signals, frequent visitors to Richmond from nearby Catterick. The material is a russet-coloured sandstone.

The Richmondshire District Council, as (reviving an ancient name) it is now called, has not only bought the station but over two miles of the former track as well, which has been turned into a public footpath: perhaps the most agreeable way, in fact, of getting from Richmond to Easby Abbey. Full marks again to the Council. Why is not this done far more often?

It would be a pleasure to be able to say that everything that has happened at Richmond in recent years was as commendable as this. Unhappily this is not possible. Since the beginning of the present century, the population has roughly doubled. It is now about 7800. So there has been much new building. But if houses *have* to look commonplace, should they not be decently concealed? Between the wars there was no planning legislation, and, across the river, unworthy villas, one group in particular, go far towards

27. St James's Chapel Wynd

28. *20–22*
Newbiggin

spoiling the view of everyone in Richmond whose windows face south-east. But a recent development has been still worse. Prominently sited on the hill to the north is a large group of new houses which seriously compromise every view in that direction. It is mystifying that planning permission should ever have been given for such architectural eyesores, so manifestly constructed of the wrong materials.

From these it is a relief to turn to St James's Chapel Wynd at the bottom of Cravengate (27), an admirable example of recent Council housing carried out almost entirely in the local stone: a mixture of sandstone, limestone and river cobbles, which very obviously 'belongs'. Equally commendable was a Corporation enterprise in 1965 in Newbiggin, where special vigilance is essential, since, strikingly broad and cobbled throughout, this is Richmond's finest street. Two houses in a bad state of decay were taken down and rebuilt as six flats. Much of the stone used for these two houses would seem originally to have come from the river. It was all salvaged and re-used on the new rubblestone front (28), and scrupulous adherence was also given to the street's building and roof lines.

Preserve what is worth preserving. Watch the building lines. Wherever possible, use local materials. And avoid naked concrete. Those are some of the precepts to follow if we want to ensure that old towns like Richmond shall continue to look worthy of their past.

29. The Market Place in 1944

TEWKESBURY

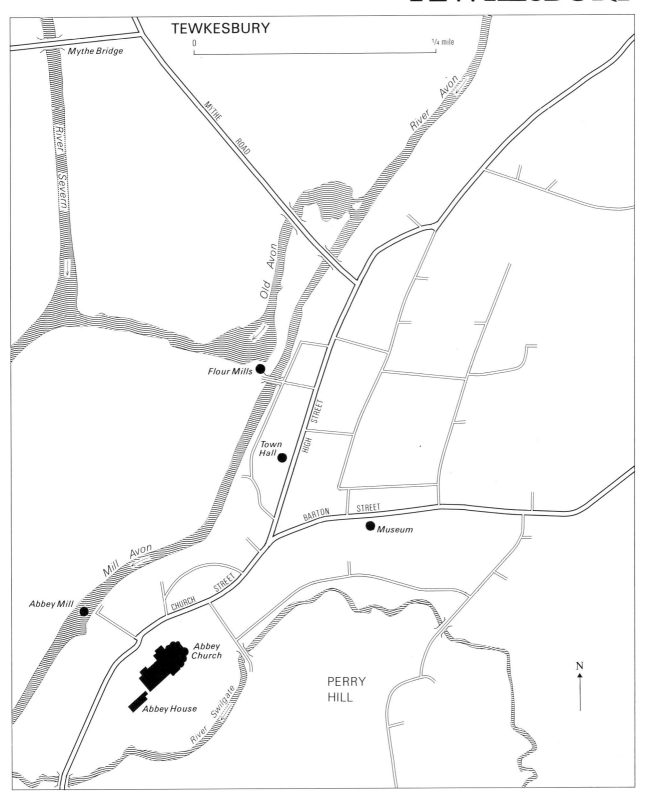

TEWKESBURY

0   ¼ mile

Mythe Bridge

River Avon

MYTHE ROAD

River Severn

Old Avon

Flour Mills

HIGH STREET

Town Hall

BARTON STREET

Museum

Mill Avon

CHURCH STREET

Abbey Mill

Abbey Church

Abbey House

River Swilgate

PERRY HILL

N

1. *Tewkesbury – town plan*

Tewkesbury existed in Anglo-Saxon times, and in 800 one of the West Saxon Kings, Brictric, was buried here, in the first Abbey; but during the ninth century the Danes several times sailed up the Severn and plundered the monastery, which by 1000 had only five monks. Soon after this its status was reduced to that of a cell of Cranborne Abbey in Dorset. So Saxon Tewkesbury is unimportant, and nothing survives.

At the end of the eleventh century the feudal lord was Robert FitzHamon, a cousin of William Rufus. In 1102 he and Girald, the Abbot of Cranborne, decided – why is not known – to erect a new abbey church at Tewkesbury and to reduce Cranborne to priory status. The great new church was consecrated in 1121. So the town sprang up in the twelfth century, in the first place to serve the Benedictine monastery, whose church is still Tewkesbury's principal building. Among the English churches which are not cathedrals only Westminster Abbey and Beverley Minster are finer. It is predominantly a building of the twelfth and fourteenth centuries. From the earlier period the principal survivals are the tower (2), one of the largest and noblest built by the Normans (it once carried a wooden spire); the west front (4), the centre part of which steps forward no fewer than six times, in ever bolder and loftier arches; and, within, the huge circular piers of the nave (7), each $6\frac{1}{4}$ ft in diameter and nearly 31 ft high. In the twelfth century similar naves were built at Pershore and at Evesham, but today only the nave of Gloucester Cathedral is comparable.

3. *The Abbey from the south-east*

For their continuing prosperity, all the medieval monasteries were largely dependent upon benefactors: and here Tewkesbury was lucky. A succession of noble patrons were lavish with their endowments: in the thirteenth century the De Clares, in the fourteenth the Despensers, and in the fifteenth the Beauchamps. All these in turn held the honour

4. *The West front*

of Tewkesbury, an honour, in feudal times, being a group of manors held under one
baron or lord: so they could well afford to give. But few monastic foundations received
so much.

Eleanor, the last of the De Clares, married Hugh le Despenser, who, like the King,
Edward II, with whom he had been much involved, was murdered. As a memorial to
him, she gave the seven big windows of fourteenth-century stained glass in the clere-
story of the sanctuary. Only the central window, the one facing east, has a subject: here
is the Last Judgment, with the Resurrection below. Otherwise, each light has just a
single figure: in the two eastern pairs, kings and prophets (6); in the western pair,
knights connected with Tewkesbury, clad in armour and helms and wearing surcoats
that are mainly yellow and red, against backgrounds of rich greens patterned with con-
ventionalised flowers (5). Boldly designed figures like these are absolutely right for this
lofty situation. Although the facial features are rendered with strength and conviction,
they are not portraits. Only the arms on their surcoats identify them.

Like most Norman churches, Tewkesbury only had a wooden roof. The vault was given by Eleanor's son and daughter-in-law, Hugh le Despenser the younger and Elizabeth Montacute (who completed the work after his death in 1348). In the nave the vault, although fine in itself, is too low: it seems rammed down on to the great Norman piers like a lid. But east of the crossing the church was reconstructed in the fourteenth century, to its great architectural advantage (8). Here the vault, built of Cotswold limestone, is among the most perfect in England: a glorious enrichment. This is a lierne

7. The nave looking west

8. *The sanctuary*

vault – from the French word *lier*, to tie. The liernes are the short ribs which tie the main ones together, to produce an exquisitely ornamental design (31). At every point of junction is a carved boss, and all these bosses were originally painted and gilded. Then, after the battle of Tewkesbury in 1471 (the door of the sacristy is still covered with armour-plate – arm- and leg-pieces – taken from soldiers lying dead on the battlefield), the Yorkists commemorated their victory over the Lancastrians by adding their emblem, a circle of gilded suns. What a lovely gesture!

Many of these grandees chose to be buried in the Abbey: some have not just tombs but chantry chapels. So fine indeed are the monuments here that Tewkesbury has been aptly described as 'the Westminster Abbey of the feudal baronage'. The best of all is that of the Despensers, Hugh and Elizabeth, which was clearly inspired by the even finer monument to Edward II at Gloucester. Here they lie, side by side, carved in alabaster (9): he, as so often, with a lion at his feet and she with a dog. The tabernacle which envelops them is believed to be of Beer limestone from Devon, brought here because it lends itself, as does no Cotswold stone, to the most intricate detail. It has not, alas, escaped the attentions of the vandals or of the religious fanatics: not one of a score or more of its statuettes has been permitted to survive. But even now it is one of the loveliest English monuments of the Middle Ages: delicate, complicated, subtle (10).

9. *Hugh and Elizabeth le Despenser*

At the Dissolution the town, to its eternal honour, paid Henry VIII £453 – a big sum in those days, equivalent to at least £60,000 today – to acquire the monastic parts. So the abbey church, now parish church, survives almost intact (3), a grand brooding presence

10. *Hugh le Despenser's monument*

11. *The Abbey Gatehouse*

constantly in view. Incidentally, it was with reference to this church that, in March 1877, William Morris wrote his famous letter protesting against mischievous over-restoration, which not only stopped it here but led to the foundation of that splendid body, the Society for the Protection of Ancient Buildings.

Everyone will be struck by the contrast between the church, which is built entirely of stone, and the town, in which stone is the exception. Nearly all the stone, oolitic limestone, came from quarries to the east of Tewkesbury: some from Bredon hill, which was the nearest (six to seven miles) and the rest from various quarries in the Cotswolds, not all of which have been identified. These might have been fifteen miles away: not an easy journey, although it was at least all downhill or on the level. In the twelfth century a little stone appears to have been brought from Caen, while for those parts of the tower formerly masked by steep roofs they brought sandstone, also by water, from the Forest of Dean.

Tewkesbury's other stone buildings are few, and nearly all close to the Abbey. There is the handsome early Tudor Gatehouse (11), faced with that unmistakably yellow limestone from Guiting in the Cotswolds. Next to it is the only other conventual building to have survived: Abbey House, formerly the Abbot's lodging or perhaps his guest house, and now the Vicarage. This, in its structure, is a fascinating mixture. Internally it can be seen to be still largely timber-framed, while the garden front, giving on to (and darkened by) a venerable cedar tree, is Georgian and of brick. But the north side, facing the churchyard, is of stone (12): there is a beautiful early Tudor oriel window in Cotswold oolite, but otherwise the walling is blue lias. It came from Twyning, two miles to the north, so this is Tewkesbury's only truly local stone; but it is so soft that it has decayed badly, and it would seem that hardly anybody else considered it to be worth using.

12. *Abbey House*

Across the churchyard is the former National School, begun in 1813, probably in Painswick stone, also from the Cotswolds. Almost the only other stone building is the Town Hall, built originally in 1788 but twice altered in the Victorian period. Both these

13 *(far left).
The Abbey mill*

14 *(left). The
churchyard gates*

are buildings of some distinction, but untypical of Tewkesbury, as, I feel, are the grandly ceremonial wrought-iron gates to the churchyard, presented in 1734 by Lord Gage, which were perhaps the work of William Edney, the leading smith of Bristol (14).

From the top of the Abbey tower, all of 205 steps up, the view is revealing. Until the Industrial Revolution a river was nearly always the key to an inland town's prosperity. When roads were bad, and in winter sometimes impassable, barges were the only convenient way of transporting bulky goods. For water transport Tewkesbury was very well sited, for only half a mile away across the meadows to the left there is another and much larger river, the Severn, into which, a short distance downstream, the Avon flows.

It may seem odd that the town was not built at the junction of the two rivers. The reason, which still applies, is because of flooding. Valley-beds were much more often water-logged in the Middle Ages than they are today; but even now the whole of these pastures is sometimes under water. That is why they are so lush. Such fertile land was excellent for corn growing, and corn was always important here. In fact, as early as the twelfth century the Avon was diverted to provide power for the Abbey mill.

The original water mill does not of course survive. What we see now is a late eighteenth-century replacement, with a weather-boarded addition not even as old as that (13). It is no longer used for its original purpose, nor are the malthouse and granary adjoining, which incorporate remains of the Abbey barn. But today there is another flour mill by the Avon that is far and away the biggest industrial building in the town.

Apart from corn, the principal industries before the seventeenth century were wool and the weaving of cloth. From the earliest days Tewkesbury also had a flourishing market. And William Camden, writing in 1586, tells us that this place was famous, too, for its smart, biting mustard. In fact, if you wanted to suggest that somebody was very strong, there was an old saying: 'He looks as if he lives on Tewkesbury mustard'.

15. *View from the Abbey tower*

The town had rather an odd plan: long and narrow, with the three principal streets forming a Y (1). The reason was that it could not expand westwards across the Avon, nor even on the land immediately to the south of the Abbey, because of the danger of floods. And towards the east it was hemmed in by abbey lands and the manorial estate. So even in the Middle Ages this was always a congested place, densely built up (15). It was shortage of space which accounts for a special feature of Tewkesbury: the alleys. A good many still survive. Some are so narrow that upstairs the buildings on either side can be seen to be almost touching (16). And down the alleys, behind the main street houses, there might be a lofty hall: a workshop perhaps, or a barn.

Until the closing years of the seventeenth century Tewkesbury was a timber-framed town, and survivors are still plentiful. The most familiar is the House of the Nodding Gables, or of the Golden Key, in the High Street (17): one of those faintly intoxicated-looking buildings, with overhanging upper storeys – no fewer than four of them here – making their obeisance to passers-by. Here, it is true, the gables nod more than usual, the result of an accident. The ridge-pieces broke and had to be secured.

Apart from their undeniable picturesqueness, it used to be said that the chief reason why jetties were so popular was that they gave people more floor space upstairs – which is certainly true. In towns pinched for space like Tewkesbury, they would no doubt have been very welcome. Yet in fact the justification of the jetty was purely structural. Think of upstairs rooms full of furniture: heavy oak beds, tables, chests and so on. In due course the joists that carry these heavy pieces will be almost certain to sag. But if these joists project into space and are weighted at their outer ends by having to carry upper walls and part of the roof, the effect is one of counterpoise. Thus a jetty is actually a source not of weakness but of strength. Nor should it be forgotten that in the sixteenth century, when many of those houses went up, there were no gutters and no downpipes. The rain just poured off the roof. Lime-plaster is very vulnerable to rainwater. The jetties were also useful, therefore, in helping to throw the water clear of the walls. That in the process it spouted instead upon the heads of the passers-by was just too bad.

16 (far left).
Ancil's Court

17 (left).
The House of
the Nodding
Gables, an early
photograph

In Tudor and Jacobean days the timbers would seem never to have been black. A permanent black was not to be had until tar and pitch, distilled from coal, became available, and that was associated with the industrial processes of the nineteenth century. When early oak timbers, later plastered over, are revealed again, the oak is always found to be in its natural state: that is to say, light brown or grey brown. 'Black and white', which we associate mainly with the western counties and with the North, was essentially a Victorian fashion. It became so popular that sometimes, as can be seen at 22 Barton Street, the timbers, or at least some of them, are a sham, just painted on to brick.

My own decided preference is for the oak to be left in its natural state, unblacked. That is what we find at 64 Barton Street, a seventeenth-century house carefully restored to serve as a museum. The special feature of this house is the continuous range of sixteen casement windows with leaded lights on the first floor (18).

In the recent restoration of a long range of late-medieval houses now known as Abbey Cottages, in that part of Church Street backing on to the Abbey, it is a pity that thick, wooden glazing bars were introduced instead, for these do not look right, and here the oak timbers have been so drastically limewashed as to present a positively bleached appearance. With these two provisos the work can be warmly applauded. At a cost exceeding £100,000, a range which had become so dilapidated as to be in serious danger of demolition, on a site of vital importance to the town, has been saved for posterity (19). In the Georgian period two of the houses had been wholly, and two more partly, refronted: the former, quite rightly, have not been altered.

19. *Abbey Cottages*

Clarence House in the High Street, also late-medieval in origin, was reconstructed about 1630, when it lost two of its three original gables. But at that time was inserted, on the first floor, the finest plaster ceiling in Tewkesbury. With its wreaths, cherubs and central raspberry pendant, and its acanthus-leaf cornice with egg and dart mouldings, this ceiling is surprisingly sumptuous for so modest a house.

After the monastery was dissolved in 1539, the town, which so largely depended on it, lost a good deal of its prosperity, and it was not until the Georgian period that it really began to pick up again. The corn trade was still important, and so now were malting and leather goods, especially saddles; but there was no more cloth-weaving. Instead, the people took to knitting, which was done at home on frames. In 1723, Daniel Defoe, following the Severn from Gloucester, 'came to Tewksbury (sic), a large and very populous town, . . . famous for a great manufacture of stockings'. This was still true a century later, when one inhabitant in every four was knitting stockings.

Another flourishing industry now was brickmaking. Beside the Severn, where there was plenty of suitable clay, both above and below the town brickworks were started. So timber went right out. By the early years of the eighteenth century, everyone wanted brick.

20. *79–80 Barton Street*

Not everyone, however, could afford to rebuild. A good many houses in Tewkesbury which appear to be of Georgian brick are in fact only brick-fronted. The brickwork may, in fact, only be skin deep. A closer look will sometimes suggest clues. Take 79–80 Barton Street, formerly the Star and Garter, a coaching inn (20). The brick front carries a lead rainwater head dated 1715. But the windows are not three lights across and four up, as the standard, and best, Georgian practice prescribed. They are four lights by four, and that is because of the low rooms. For these are not Georgian rooms at all: they belong to the much earlier timber-framed structure. If we step through the arch and view the building from the back, the timbers are still very much in evidence.

Georgian builders had to contend with the effects of two very troublesome taxes, of which this house also provides a good illustration. The tax on windows, which was really no more than a clumsy and extremely inept form of property tax, was first levied in 1696, and was increased no fewer than six times between 1747 and 1808: it was not finally repealed until 1851. In addition, in 1746 a heavy excise duty was imposed upon glass. So, in order to escape these taxes, the less affluent were driven to blocking up window after window. That this building in Barton Street wears today rather a starved look is because no fewer than six windows were blocked, and still are. Nevertheless, the Georgian age was a prosperous time for Tewkesbury. In just over a century the population doubled: in 1723 it was 2866; in 1831, 5780.

There are some very pleasant brick houses in Church Street, including a short Crescent, but all the best are in the High Street. It is unfortunate that the ground floors of a good many of them have had to be converted into shops or offices. Most of the pleasures now are at first- and second-floor levels. One of the most enjoyable, upstairs, is the Swan Hotel (21). The gracious sash-framed windows not only preserve all their glazing bars but their original Crown glass too.

21. *The Swan Hotel*

Early window glass, like stained glass, had been blown in cylinders or muffs, which were split along their length and flattened out as they cooled. But for Crown glass the process was quite different. The glass-blower inserted his hollow pipe (the 'blowing-iron') into the furnace and drew out a globule of molten 'metal' (as he called it). Then, taking a wooden bat and keeping the iron spinning all the time, he gradually flattened out the red-hot globule until it became a large circular disc. It must have been wonderful to watch. Because it did not come into contact with any other surfaces while it was being made, Crown glass kept a natural fire-finish, which gave it a special brilliancy, a compensation for frequent optical distortion, caused by the disc being always somewhat thicker towards the centre. (The 'bull's eye' in the middle, from which at the last moment the end of the blowing-iron would be detached, was very properly discarded in the eighteenth century.) Crown glass, confined to lights of Georgian proportions, can often be identified by its glinting reflections. But for more than a century it has been unobtainable, having been completely supplanted by machine-produced glass in sheets large enough to need no glazing bars, which appeared just in time for the Crystal Palace of 1851.

We only have to walk along the High Street at Tewkesbury to realise what a wretched aesthetic deprivation the removal of Georgian glazing bars and the substitution of sheet glass have entailed. Kingsbury House (Nos. 39–40) (24), Avonside (No.63) (22) and

22. *Avonside, High Street*

Riverside House (No. 66) (23) are all excellent examples of eighteenth-century brickwork. But at Kingsbury House all the windows except the two in the so-called Venetian style in the centre have been spoilt: the window openings are no more than dark, cavernous holes in the wall, featureless and devoid of character. At the other two houses the damage has fortunately been confined to the ground-floor windows, but even this is serious. At both these some compensation is provided by the unusual character of the fanlights over the doors.

A special feature of Tewkesbury's Georgian buildings is the key-block of moulded terracotta over the centre of each window. These blocks, which were usually painted white, display a variety of decorative motifs.

All these houses belong to the years of Tewkesbury's greatest prosperity, and provide a perfect foil to the less sophisticated character of much of the half-timbering.

Within, too, there are survivals of Georgian elegance. The Tudor House Hotel (No. 52), despite the handsome castellated-lead rainwater heads dated 1701, has a front disfigured with mock timber-framing in 1897 (26). It is therefore a delightful surprise, on entering, to find a very handsome Georgian staircase of impeccable proportions (25).

23. *Riverside House (now Hotel), High Street*

At last, about 1800, the condition of the roads began to improve, and brought an influx of new traffic. Tewkesbury had always been on the direct north-south route from the Midlands to Bristol, but up to this time the rivers were usually preferred for the transport of merchandise, and sometimes by travellers too. But, in addition to better

24 *(opposite). Kingsbury House, High Street*

roads, a great change was brought about in 1826 by the bridging of the Severn, where previously there had only been a ferry.

The designer of the Mythe Bridge was Thomas Telford, the greatest bridge-builder of the age. Before he was brought upon the scene in 1823, it was intended to have three arches. Telford found that the river bed was nothing but soft alluvial clay, so declared that the only solution was a single span. His design was carried out to the letter. The span is 170 feet, and on either side, he wrote, 'is a series of open arches, in place of solid masonry. I was led to this from having observed, in all the other cast-iron bridges constructed under my direction, that the great mass of solid masonry in the wings did not accord well with the openness of the ironwork; these arches are also of use when the floods rise more than three feet above the springing . . . As this is the first instance in which this mode has been adopted, I reckon this the handsomest bridge which has been built under my direction'[1] (27, 28).

[1]This quotation is taken from *A History of Tewkesbury* by James Bennett (1830: reprinted by Alan Sutton, 1976), pp. 288–9.

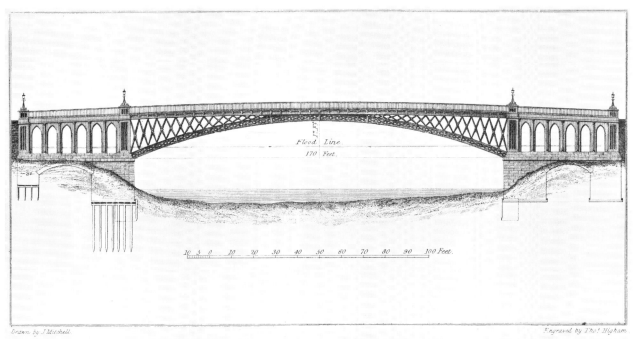

Drawn by J. Mitchell.   Engraved by Thos. Higham.

TEWKESBURY SEVERN BRIDGE.

Designed by Thomas Telford, F.R.S.E.

27, 28. *The Mythe Bridge and Telford's design for it*

29. *The old Grammar School*

Since the year 1826 had already seen, on 30 January, the opening of a far more remarkable bridge by Telford, the Suspension Bridge over the Menai Straits, with a central span of 579 feet, which was easily the greatest in the world at that time, it is perhaps surprising that the opening of the Mythe Bridge should have been greeted with such excitement. Six years later the Grosvenor Bridge over the Dee at Chester, designed in 1827 by the veteran architect Thomas Harrison, was to achieve a span of 200 feet *in stone*, and to become, what it still remains, the boldest masonry arch in the kingdom. But at Tewkesbury Telford used cast iron, which, like the stone for the abutments, was floated down the river from Shropshire. The bridge brought the east-west traffic, going to Ledbury and Hereford. By 1830 thirty stage-coaches a day were either arriving at Tewkesbury or passing through. The House of the Nodding Gables became the ticket office for them. The inns flourished as never before.

But when, a few years later, the Birmingham to Bristol railway was built, it by-passed Tewkesbury and went through Ashchurch, where to this day many Tewkesbury people go to work. It is only two miles away, but that was far enough to result in the Industrial Revolution giving Tewkesbury a miss. The population in 1931 was actually 1400 less than a hundred years earlier. So there was practically no new building here between 1850 and 1930, which was visually, of course, a great piece of luck.

One building like the former Grammar School, now the Public Library (29), is surely quite enough – and all the more so as, by ill-fortune, it is situated nearly opposite the Abbey. It is built of machine-pressed bricks, probably from Ruabon – bricks made of hard, carbonaceous clay, faultless in their precision, relentless in their durability, pitiless in their colour. Needless to say these harsh reds were pointed with dark mortar. The machine-made tiles are equally rebarbative, while the typical cresting and the pair of cowls supply the final *coup de grâce*.

But there is an early Victorian façade in Tewkesbury which is very likeable: No. 124 High Street (30). The original house goes back to 1606 (hence the date above the

30. *124 High Street*

window), but in 1845 it was given a new front, in Gothick. The facing material is stucco, painted grey and white.

Since the last war, Tewkesbury has again become prosperous. (In 1981 the population was 9554.) This has brought with it one absolutely deplorable development in the High Street, carried out just before the whole of the old town was very properly designated a Conservation Area. But by and large the character of the place has been well preserved, and, perhaps partly owing to the diversion of much of the through traffic on to the M5 a mile and a half to the east, the buildings seem to be better maintained now than they used to be.

The appeal largely depends upon materials: the right materials in the right place. Oaks from nearby woods for timber-framing. Clay from the banks of the Severn for brick-making. Stone only for a few of the less private edifices: the Town Hall, the National School, the Gatehouse, and above all, of course, for the Abbey church, to which, here at Tewkesbury, our eyes and our thoughts continually return.

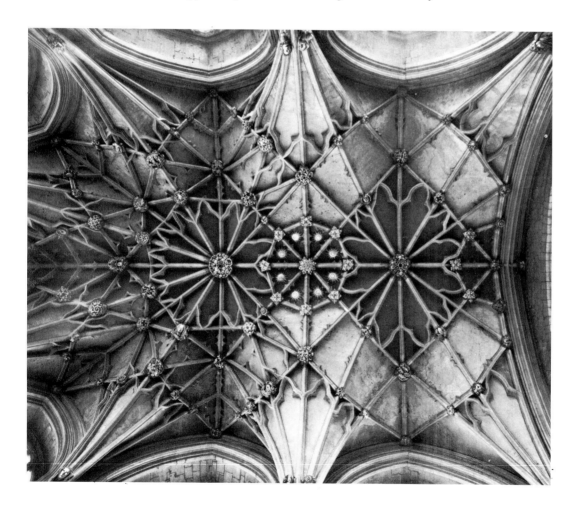

31. *Sanctuary vault, Tewkesbury Abbey*

STAMFORD

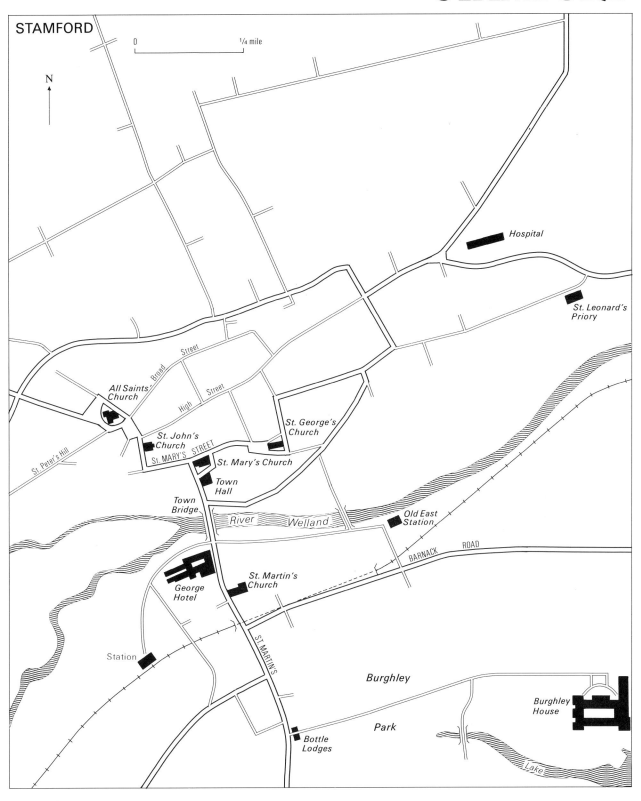

STAMFORD

0 — 1/4 mile

N

Hospital

St. Leonard's Priory

Broad Street

All Saints' Church

High Street

St. John's Church

St. George's Church

St. Peter's Hill

St. MARY'S STREET

St. Mary's Church

Town Hall

Town Bridge

River Welland

Old East Station

BARNACK ROAD

George Hotel

St. Martin's Church

Station

ST MARTIN'S

Burghley

Park

Bottle Lodges

Burghley House

Lake

1. *Stamford – town plan*

'Stone ford' it was originally, then 'Stanford'. The implication is clear. It came into being as the place at which the Welland could most conveniently be forded. Both above and below the town the river is alluvial and in rainy seasons would be marshy: even today it is very prone to flooding. Here, between low hills, the valley contracts and the river bed is of limestone. When the ford was first replaced by a bridge is not known, but it was not later than 1086, and may well have been a long time before then.

There was, however, no Roman settlement here, although Ermine Street passed only a few hundred yards to the west. The small Roman town which grew up around a first-century fort was at Great Casterton, a couple of miles north-west.

Stamford was first settled by the Saxons. But in the ninth century it fell to the Danes and became one of the five *burhs* (or Boroughs) of the Danelaw (the others being Lincoln, Nottingham, Derby and Leicester). About 920 the town was recovered by the Anglo-Saxons, and a period of considerable prosperity ensued. It minted its own coins, and under Edgar (959–975) was ranked fifth among the English towns. By the time of the Domesday survey in 1086, the population was about 3000.

Despite the absence of any cathedral or large abbey or priory, the Church was very strong in Stamford throughout the Middle Ages. There were eleven parish churches within the walled town, another just outside to the east, and two more in Stamford Baron, south of the Welland. In addition, all the four principal mendicant orders – Dominicans (Black friars), Franciscans (Grey), Carmelites (White) and Austin friars – had houses here, and monasteries throughout England owned property in Stamford.

Why? Probably because the town had unusually good schools, and even, for a few years early in the fourteenth century, the beginnings of a university. Royal intervention (by Edward III) was needed, at the urgent prompting of Oxford and Cambridge, to suppress what threatened to become another university here. But the undoubted prosperity of Stamford in the Middle Ages depended almost entirely upon trade. Geography was very kind to this town. To the east lay the Fens, which yielded thousands of waterfowl and a profusion of fish, especially eels. In every other direction there were abundant grasslands: Northamptonshire, Rutland and Leicestershire were all great wool-producing areas, and Lincolnshire was well known for the quality of its fleeces. Originally most of this wool went to Flanders, but early in the thirteenth century cloth-making was started in England; and very fine cloth it was. Stamford's worsteds became famous. Other local industries flourished, notably pottery, tanning, iron-founding and smelting and stone-quarrying, while the town was also an important market for agricultural produce; but the poll-tax returns for 1379 leave no room for doubt that the wool merchants were predominant.

Then, in 1461, Stamford suffered a misfortune. As the Lancastrians, an army of rough northerners and Scotsmen, passed through on their way south, they are said to have sacked and burned this Yorkist town. Whether they did as much damage as used to be believed has recently been questioned,[1] but the fact remains that, apart from five churches, all considerably restored, Stamford preserves remarkably little from its flourishing medieval past.

The walls have almost gone, and so, long ago, have all the gates. The small castle built during the reign of William the Conqueror and probably rebuilt about 1210 was already in ruins by 1340, and the remains are insignificant. St Leonard's Priory has fared only a little better. This was a cell of Durham, erected about 1090 outside the walls. The north arcade of the nave survives, very plain, and so does most of the west front, rebuilt about 1150 (3): here, although it is unfortunate that the doorway has been walled up, the carved ornamentation is quite rich. This is the best place in Stamford to see Barnack ragstone.

3. *St Leonard's Priory*

Barnack, which is three and a half miles east of Stamford, had one of the largest and most famous quarries of the Middle Ages. Cathedrals, abbeys, priories and many parish churches in eastern England, large and small, were built of its stone; originally all those at Stamford were. It is a coarse-grained Jurassic limestone, very hard and durable. But before the end of the fourteenth century the best beds had been worked out. All Stamford's five surviving medieval churches were extensively or entirely rebuilt between 1450 and 1500. For this, therefore, the local Stamford stone, also excellent, replaced the Barnack rag, and during the nineteenth century other limestones were employed for repairs and additions, including Ketton, Clipsham and Ancaster.

[1]See *The Town of Stamford* (Royal Commission on Historical Monuments, 1977), pp. xlii and xlvi.

None of Stamford's churches can be described as outstanding, but happily their towers and spires still dominate the skyline (4, 38). Entering the town from the south, St Martin comes first, with its Perpendicular tower rising to a sumptuous crown: there are battlements pierced with quatrefoils and lofty crocketed pinnacles (5). Across the Welland St Mary, with its stately tower, of *c.* 1220, and spire added about a century

4. *Stamford from the south-west*

5.
J. M. W. Turner, St Martin's, *c. 1829*

later and rising to 160 feet, occupies a commanding site (2). Then, following the extraordinary 'dog-leg' course of the old Great North Road, so improbable and still so inconvenient, but accounted for by the continuing presence within the medieval town of the walled circuit of the old Danish *burh*, we pass St John the Baptist, with angel roofs, and arrive at All Saints' (7). This occupies an island site and from the Early English period has, externally on the south and east sides, delightful blind arcading with moulded arches and detached colonnettes (6) and, within, a beautiful south arcade with clustered piers. It also has a good Perpendicular tower and spire at its north-west corner. St Martin has old glass mostly brought in 1757 from the church at Tattershall, but is chiefly notable for the imposing monuments of the Cecils.

6. *Arcading on the south side of All Saints' church*

For more than four centuries the Cecils, Earls and later Marquesses of Exeter, have been closely identified with Stamford, politically, economically – for despite many sales they still have a substantial interest as landlords – and in their contribution to the preservation of the town as we see it today.

   The first member of the family to achieve eminence was William, Lord Burghley, who was Lord Treasurer and Secretary of State to Elizabeth I until his death in 1598. He was buried in the church of St Martin. Although limestone was the material of many medieval church monuments, from the fourteenth century grand people began to prefer English alabaster for their effigies. One of the earliest is that of Prince John of Eltham, who died in 1334, in Westminster Abbey. Another early pair we have already encountered: Hugh and Elizabeth le Despenser at Tewkesbury. By the middle of the sixteenth century, alabaster had largely supplanted limestone for the effigies of people of importance. So, needless to say, Burghley is in this material. The rest of the monument is made of variously-coloured imported marbles (8). It occupies the whole of the first bay to the left of the altar.

8. *William Cecil's monument in St Martin's church*

7. *All Saints' church*

9. *John and Anne Cecil's monument in St Martin's church*

A century later, marble was virtually the only acceptable material for the grander monuments. A striking example in the north chapel of the same church, dated 1704, commemorates John Cecil, fifth Earl of Exeter, and his wife Anne Cavendish, with flanking figures standing for Victory and the Arts (9). The sculptor, who worked in Rome, was Stephen Monnet. It is heartless but immensely accomplished and self-assured.

Symbolically, nevertheless, William Cecil should have been commemorated in limestone, for at the Dissolution it was he who acquired from the Abbot of Peterborough the quarries at Barnack. And although by this time the ragstone quarries were worked out (or very nearly so), two other varieties were now exploited. To the north-west of the village they found an oolite of a finer grain with small shell fragments, which lent itself to excellent ashlar; whereas, in complete contrast, a hard-rubble limestone, still being quarried almost until 1900, was good for rough local work.

It was the fine oolite which was principally used for the prodigious mansion which Lord Burghley had built for himself only a mile and a half from the town centre (11). When Defoe saw it about 1724, he said:

It looks more like a town than a house; the towers and the pinnacles so high, and placed at such a distance from one another, look like so many distant parish-churches in a great town, and a large spire covered with lead,[1] over the great clock in the centre, looks like the cathedral or chief church of the town.

10. *The Bottle Lodges, Burghley Park*

Celia Fiennes thought Burghley House 'eminent for its Curiosity', which it certainly is; William III termed it 'too great for a subject', which, having regard to the cost of maintaining a house such as this today, is equally true. But the State Rooms have

[1]Here Defoe was in error. The obelisk-like spire is and was always stone.

11. Burghley House from the north-west

been regularly open to visitors since 1798, and parts of the park are also always accessible to the public.

Burghley Park (12) is one of the masterpieces of Capability Brown: the date is about 1760. As usual with him, we do not look for colour. He worked with trees and water; the trees here are mainly limes, chestnuts – both the horse and the Spanish, beeches and oaks. Luckily for Burghley, there were never many elms. To Brown is also due the lovely serpentine lake. He never went in much for temples, but he loved a stone bridge, and this lake has a very graceful example, in Stamford stone (13).

At the town entrance to the park are what are popularly known as the Bottle Lodges (10). They were designed in 1801 by William Daniel Legge, a freeman of Stamford, who thought the design worth exhibiting that year at the Royal Academy. They are delightful, and the masoncraft, which is in Ketton stone, the finest of all Stamford's local materials, is superb.

Few great estates are closer to their towns than Burghley is to Stamford (1). Yet so well screened is it by belts of trees, another of the special characteristics of Brown's parks, that, were it not for the Bottle Lodges, the unknowing visitor would be likely to pass by quite unaware of its existence. Only on the Barnack road can the mansion be glimpsed from no great distance, at the head of a long, straight avenue.

At the time when William Cecil was building his palatial house, the contrast between his own colossal fortune and the plight of the town must have been not a little poignant. A place so dependent on the strength and goodwill of the Church could not but be seriously affected by the Reformation. The wool trade had also declined sharply. 'The old upright loom became obsolete with the introduction of a new luxury cloth, close woven and fluffy, which was produced on a horizontal loom, in which Stamford was unable to participate.'[1] And about the same time a still worse misfortune occurred: the Welland silted up. The wool and the cloth had all been shipped by water; the river was no longer navigable. In about 1570 an Act was obtained to remedy this, but for fifty years nothing was done. With houses empty and neglected and some churches falling into disuse, the population had dropped to no more than 1500. 'A poor decayed town' was how Lord Keeper Lincoln described it in 1624.

But one factor did not change: the excellence of the local building stone. Within a four-mile radius of the town, in almost every direction, were quarries of Jurassic limestone. Among three that have already been mentioned are two of the most famous in England: Barnack and Ketton. The third was Stamford's own quarry, which supplied nearly all the town's needs from the fifteenth to the early part of the nineteenth century – a fine stone only a mile away, and all downhill. At Wittering the quarry yielded a stone called pendle, of which there will be more to say presently. But that is not all. Only just

12 (*opposite*).
Burghley Park

13 (*opposite*).
*The Bridge,
Burghley Park*

[1]Christine M. Mahany, *The Archaeology of Stamford* (1969), p. 9.

over three miles south-west of Stamford is Collyweston, which for centuries provided the most beautiful roofing material of the Midlands, still not wholly unobtainable. And excellent roofing slates were also produced in Easton-on-the-Hill, which is still nearer.

Yet even at Stamford it was cheaper, in the Middle Ages, to build with wood; at that time, therefore, most of the houses were timber-framed. So were the very few houses erected between the Reformation and the Commonwealth. Not many of these houses survive, and those with timbers exposed can almost be numbered today on the fingers of one hand. Elsewhere, however, as at 8 St Mary's Hill, a jetty plastered over gives the game away (14). For in the Georgian age, when timbering became unfashionable and new buildings were nearly all of stone, rendering was the rule. Often, too, the jetty would be underbuilt in stone, to provide more room downstairs. At one house at least, the original oak frame has in recent years been revealed again (15); but exposed timbers do not suit this town, any more than does red brick, of which happily there is also in the historic town very little: none, in fact, earlier than 1750.

With the advent of the seventeenth century Stamford began to recover, slowly at first but after the Restoration much more rapidly. The great event was the construction of 'the Welland Navigation', a $9\frac{1}{2}$-mile canal on the north side of the Welland from the eastern side of Stamford to Deeping St James. There were no fewer than twelve locks. In a life of about two hundred years – for it was not finally abandoned, a victim of rail transport, until 1863 – this canal proved of great benefit to the town. Stone and stone slates, malt and agricultural produce travelled downstream; in the opposite direction came coal, general groceries and timber, for the storage of which a large building was erected at Bath Row. The dredging of parts of the river itself during the reign of Charles II ensured a good supply of water for the mills.

14 (far left).
8 St Mary's Hill

15 (left).
6 St Peter's Hill

16. *The George*

In this new period of prosperity there was nothing in the least comparable with the former predominance of woollen cloth. But the leather and fibre industries now flourished, as did the curing and working of hides and skins from the backs of Midland cattle and sheep; hemp-weaving and rope-making too. A little later came the malting of locally grown barley: some of the former maltings still survive. Stamford also prospered again as the market town for local farm produce.

The eighteenth and especially the early nineteenth centuries were the heyday of the coaching inns. It was in 1658 that the first long-distance coach was advertised, to run from the George Inn in London's Aldersgate to Stamford in two days and on to York in two more. For many years, however, the services had to be suspended whenever heavy

rain caused flooding or rendered the road impassable. It was the establishment of Turnpike Trusts from 1738 onwards which enabled tolls to be collected from road users to provide funds for improvements; and by 1769 Stamford was linked with London via Royston by a coach making the journey in a single day. In 1792 this became a daily service.

The coaching trade reached its peak in 1830, when every day Stamford saw thirty stage and forty mail coaches stopping or passing through. Even though, until the opening of the present Town Bridge in 1848, the width of the road was no more than eight feet, Stamford's situation at a river crossing of the Great North Road was a great boon to it. Just by the bridge was the most famous inn of any, the George (16), parts of which date back to 1597. Another old inn which still survives is St Mary's Vaults, formerly the Eagle and Child. This is in origin still older.

Thus it was that after the Restoration nearly the whole town came gradually to be rebuilt, and in stone. We have seen how fortunately placed Stamford was in this respect. So stone-quarrying and masoncraft flourished now as never before. Progress must have been rapid, for despite the fact that the great majority of houses, or at least house-fronts, that can be seen today are Georgian, already by 1697 Celia Fiennes could say that Stamford was 'as fine a built town all of stone as may be seen . . . not very large but much finer than Cambridge', while in 1724 Defoe could call it 'a very fair, well-built, considerable and wealthy town'. From 1698 those who were prepared to pay the charge could even have water piped to their houses; the water was pumped from the river to cisterns, and in St Paul's Street one old conduit still survives, although of course no longer used.

Since the Georgian age stone has been so pervasive at Stamford that the contrasts are not so much between one material and another as between rubblestone and ashlar or freestone: stone, that is, which can be cut freely, either, until recently, with a hand-saw, or with a mallet and chisel. A good many buildings, like 15 Broad Street (17), show both: ashlar in front and rubblestone at the sides (where visible) and behind. Ashlar cost more – the term implies a smooth surface, but often no more than a facing: slabs of stone fairly thin but frequently quite large, carefully squared and finely jointed in level courses. For this Stamford's oolitic limestone is ideal.

Much of this stone, it must be said, is now badly in need of cleaning (17–19, 21–23,

18. 24 St Mary's Street

25, 31, 32, 36), and it is very much to be hoped that this will soon be done. The cost would not be exorbitant, for at Stamford nothing would be needed but sprays of clean, cold water and bristle brushes. (Where the limestone is harder, or very dirty indeed, a compressed-air stream with a sandy or gritty abrasive – such as is always required in the cleaning of the tougher sandstones – may be necessary.) But, as can be seen in London, Bath and elsewhere, the visual benefits are immense. The ashlar-faced houses are much the easiest to clean, and happily they are comfortably in the majority here.

From Charles II's time (the earliest important house, 19 St George's Square, dates from 1674) until the early years of Queen Victoria the style was almost consistently classical. Architecturally speaking, some of the houses here are very unspectacular, which can indeed be sometimes counted as a virtue. Unlike, say, Bath, they did not go in much here for imposing pediments nor for pilasters and engaged half-columns; and when they did, the results could be singularly unconvincing, even inept. The Stamford specialities were architraves and especially keystones. The architraves are the moulded frames which surround the windows and the door, and in this town they are usually one sixth of the width of the opening. The keystones, at their best, are tremendously robust and self-assured, especially if they date from the reign of George II.

To keep up-to-date with current architectural fashions, the local builders relied mainly upon pattern-books: the sources of some of these designs have been identified. At 25–26 High Street, for example, the architraves are not only eared (the ears are the little projecting pieces at the top) but, what is much more unusual, they step up in the centre too (19). The source of this design was Plate 45 in James Gibbs's *Rules for Drawing* (20), which had been published in 1732, just before this house was built.[1]

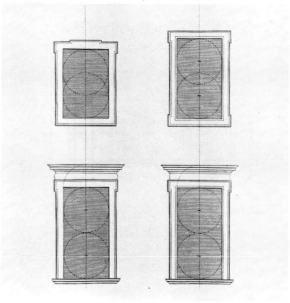

19 *(far left).* *25–26 High Street*

20 *(left).* *James Gibbs's* Rules for Drawing, *plate 45*

[1]For this reference, as for others in this essay, I am indebted to the splendid Royal Commission on Historical Monuments Inventory: *The Town of Stamford* (1977).

21 *(right).*
47 St Martin's

22 *(far right).*
66 St Martin's

23 *(right).*
13 Barn Hill

24 *(far right).*
35 St Martin's

It is evident that some of the builders enjoyed themselves very much in the treatment of keystones, which were arranged in a variety of different ways, according to carefully worked out rules. Some are single, some triple (22, 24), some quintuple (21), one (13 Barn Hill) even septemtuple (23); some widely splayed, a few fluted. The sides radiate from a common point which may be exactly in the centre of the window opening, or higher, or lower. At some houses the effect of liveliness is further enhanced by inserting blocks into the mouldings of the architraves: what Pevsner calls 'Gibbs surrounds' (31). At 21 High Street (25), the most high-spirited of all these fronts, there are fluted pilasters too, for good measure. The style might be called Jazzy Palladian – a contradiction in terms if ever there was!

At the Town Hall (26), built of Stamford stone in 1776, the ground floor is

25. 21 High Street

26. The Town Hall

rusticated: that is to say, the courses between the blocks of stone are recessed, to produce shadows and an effect of greater strength at the base. Here all the windows preserve their original glazing bars, and how immensely important, visually, that is. Fortunately a fairly high proportion of Stamford's Georgian houses keep the bars in their windows, and some have their original Crown glass too.

All these houses were roofed with Collyweston limestone slates, almost all of which still remain. To this beautiful roofing material, which varies in colour from blue-grey to brown, Stamford owes not a little of its distinction. Only limestone which is naturally fissile – that is to say, susceptible to splitting into comparatively thin pieces – is suitable

27. *16 All Saints' Place*

for roofing. To achieve this, a succession of good hard frosts is essential. The stone, known as 'log' in the trade, was dug out from shallow pits between late October and February, covered over in order to keep the quarry sap from drying out, and watered every evening from December onwards, if necessary until March. (This can now be done with sprinklers.) The force of even one sudden thaw after a hard frost could be sufficient. But recently most of the winters have been so mild that this time-old practice can no longer be relied on, which is one reason why new limestone slates are now so expensive. What can still be had at half the cost are second-hand ones. When an old building is taken down it is usually possible to save more than three quarters of the slates; luckily they last for centuries.

To lay a roof of Collywestons, though, requires both skill and artistry. For they come in many different sizes, all of which incidentally have their traditional names – mopes and mumfords, in-bows and out-bows, wibbetts, bachelors, and many more. After cliving (additional splitting), each slate has to be dressed with a hammer, and holed near its head so that it can be fixed to the roof batten. This used to be done with a sharp pointed tool known as a bill, and the slates were hung on to the roof battens with the aid of wooden pegs. Nowadays for holing they have an electric drill, and the fixing is generally done with galvanised nails.[1]

[1]Excavations at Great Casterton have revealed that the Romans made use of Collywestons for roofing. Their slates were all laid diagonally, with a hole at the upper angle. Some can be seen in Stamford's Museum.

The secret of a good roof is careful grading. The big slates, which are usually about half an inch thick and fully two feet long, are placed at the bottom, along the eaves, and they gradually get smaller and thinner as they go up (28). To get this right is no easy matter, but in Stamford, wherever we look, we see how unerringly it has been done.

Some of the roofs here are of the mansard type: 16 All Saints' Place (27), for example. A mansard roof has two pitches on each side of the ridge, the lower one much the steeper. Such roofs are not very common in England and I believe that Stamford may have more of them than any other English town. Lately yet another way has been found of using these lovely Collyweston slates. On a recent building in the High Street they have been hung vertically (30), with excellent effect.

Stamford in the eighteenth century, with its Georgian Assembly Rooms and Theatre, was very much the social centre of its area. Yet it never became a place like, say, York, in which numbers of town houses were built by the neighbouring gentry. Nearly all the Georgian houses here belonged to prosperous merchants and professional men, which explains why very few of them have much ornamentation inside. It was the front which was the principal status symbol; and some of these houses do still convey, quite vividly, a sense of gracious living. If you arrived, for example, at 3 All Saints' Place (28, 31) on your horse, there was, facing the front door, a small wrought-iron gate opening from the stone ledge upon which you dismounted. And if you arrived on foot, in days, remember, before macadamised roads, there was, built into the wall just at the bottom of the steps, a foot-scraper.

The front of this house, of about 1730, is, as we should expect, of ashlar, but what is

29. *1–2 St Mary' Hill*

30. *Collyweston slates hung vertically in the High Street*

31. *3 All Saints' Place*

rather surprising at Stamford is to find that at the end of the eighteenth century coursed rubblestone, even for quite pretentious houses like 27 St Mary's Street (32) or 1–2 St Mary's Hill (29), would seem to have become socially quite acceptable again. By comparison with the ashlared houses, they do seem to be somewhat lacking in urbanity.

At the beginning of the nineteenth century, however, another local stone was brought into use which could not be ashlared. This was the hard, close-grained fissile limestone known as pendle, which was quarried at Wittering. It is browner than the other stones used at Stamford, and somewhat darker in tone. A typical example is The Bath House, built in 1823. Now it is a private house, and, to look at, almost a folly (33).

Geologically, pendle is very like Collyweston stone, except that it cannot be split into such thin slabs. But the beds are very narrow: never more than $3\frac{1}{2}$ inches thick and sometimes as little as one inch. So, although pendle was cheaper to obtain, it was more expensive to lay, because so many courses were required. But its weathering properties are excellent. Much the largest pendle building is the Hospital, the Stamford and Rutland Infirmary as it used to be called, of 1828. The centrepiece and dressings are of Ketton stone, but most of the walling is of coursed pendle rubblestone (34).

This is a building in the neo–Tudor style, and a little later both Stamford's railway stations were designed in neo–Elizabethan, probably in deference to Burghley House. The old Midland Railway station (35), dating from 1848, is happily still in use. The former East station has been converted into a pair of private houses.

It has often been said that it was due to the opposition of the 2nd Marquess of Exeter

34. *The Hospital*

that the Great Northern Railway did not pass through Stamford, so that (to paraphrase G. K. Chesterton) Peterborough grew so big, so big, while Stamford stayed so small. But it seems clear that the railway engineers never intended that the route should pass through Stamford. It was too far west of the direct route; the terrain, as a glance at a contoured map will confirm, was more difficult; compensation would have been much heavier. The concern of the promoters was to shorten to the utmost the distance between London and Yorkshire.

The business people of Stamford naturally wanted the railway, as the 1847 files of the local paper, the *Stamford Mercury*, amply testify. Indeed, the General Election of July 1847 was largely fought here on this issue. But by then the question had in fact already been decided. A Parliamentary Committee, under the chairmanship of Sir James Buller East, had reported unanimously, and this is what Sir James said in the House of Commons on 8 June:

The Bill before us was a deviation of the Great Northern Railway . . . by way of Stamford, a great object, of course, with the people of Stamford, who by the original line were left between four and five miles from the railway. But they already have a communication with London and the south by means of another existing railway; and as the station intended for them by the Great Northern was to be upwards of a mile from the town they would gain only an advantage of three miles, whilst all the rest of England travelling on that line, and not intending to stop at Stamford, would be carried nearly two miles out of their course by the proposed deviation. . . . It was, as it were, a fair match between Stamford on one side and all England and Scotland on the other; and we thought that all England had it. . . . It was a matter of public, and not of private, interest which governed our decision.

35. *The old Midland Railway station*

Some years later, Lord Exeter was personally involved in the construction of the four-mile branch from Essendine, on the Great Northern main line to Scotland, which was opened in 1856 and closed in 1959. Earlier, he had also used his power to insist that the Midland Railway, instead of running beside the Welland, with a tiresome level-crossing at the foot of St Martin's, should be routed higher up, through a cut-and-cover tunnel under and east of this street, to the town's great benefit.

Meanwhile, Classical architecture continued to flourish at Stamford well into the nineteenth century. Barn Hill House (36) was given a new front, in an immensely authoritative and decidedly original Classical style, as late as 1843. Somewhat earlier is Rutland Terrace (37). This is one of the town's pleasantest architectural groups, with twenty houses in the Regency style, and good wrought-iron balconies, dating from about 1830. The eastern portion is faced only with stucco, but the western part has very finely jointed stone: this is Ancaster limestone from near Grantham, an unfamiliar material here. Pilasters are introduced at the centre and at the two ends, as points of punctuation, one might say.

Could any form of urban housing be more civilised than the terrace? With only two outside walls, these houses are warmer than detached buildings, while the unity of the whole makes for dignity. To me it is a great sadness that so many architects and developers would seem to have rejected terrace housing nowadays. Socially, aesthetically and economically such houses, with their own gardens, are surely far superior to

36. *Barn Hill House*

37. *Rutland Terrace*

the high-rise blocks which have destroyed the scale and ruined the skyline of so many formerly pleasant towns that merited more consideration.

That Stamford played little part in the great industrial expansion of England in the Victorian age caused some heart-aches at the time, but with hindsight must be a cause for deep thankfulness – to its citizens as to everyone else. Some factories there were, and are, for making agricultural machinery, crude-oil engines, large marine diesel engines and electrical equipment, but fortunately they were sited away from the town centre, beside the railway to Essendine; so employment was provided without any detrimental effect on the town. Another source of current activity is, once again, the wool trade. Wool is collected by lorry from a radius of anything up to eighty miles, cleaned, prepared and graded, and then dispatched to the mills of Bradford.

Today this town of over 16,000 people is full of life, and so up-to-date that, like many others, it too has its pedestrian precinct: the whole of the High Street and Ironmonger Street. Not everyone approves, but for most people this precinct has been a great boon. Elsewhere in the town there is still far too much traffic, forced to negotiate narrow and tortuous streets, and the need for an east-west by-pass is still pressing. But at least, by a fairly bold feat of road engineering, Stamford no longer has to endure the incessant stream of heavy vehicles passing up and down the Great North Road. It is good to learn that the local people were able to insist on the new river bridge being faced with stone.

In contrast to Tewkesbury, with its wide variety of building materials, here one only, Jurassic limestone, is utterly dominant. This is a place in which the buildings that are not of stone, or at least fronted with stone, or occasionally with stucco to look like stone, hardly count. I would not describe Stamford either as radiant or as seductive, although it could be made a good deal more so if its stonework were cleaned. Nor is it a town much interested in display. It has no spectacular stone buildings, like Oxford or Cambridge: no grand set-pieces, circus, crescents, squares, like Bath. Its mood is quiet; its colour, mainly a pale grey-buff, reticent. But it has great dignity. It is the fine limestone which is the key to Stamford's identity.

38. *Stamford, from the tower of St Martin*

TOTNES

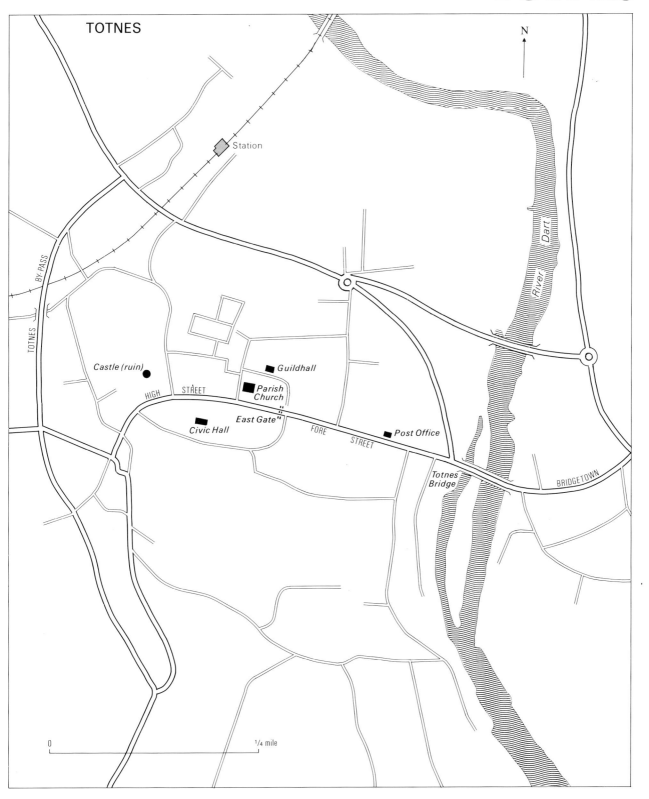

N

Station

TOTNES

TOTNES BY-PASS

River Dart

Castle (ruin)

Guildhall

HIGH STREET

Parish Church

Civic Hall

East Gate

FORE STREET

Post Office

Totnes Bridge

BRIDGETOWN

0   ¼ mile

1. *Totnes – town plan*

2. East Gate from Fore Street in 1944

Near the end of the eighth century King Alfred established in Devon four forts, to counter the menace of the Danes. The chief was Exeter: one of the other *burhs*, as they were called, was Halwell. About 950 this burh was moved five miles farther north, to a much more easily defensible site, which was Totnes.

The name derives from two Saxon words, *tot*, which means a look-out, and *nais*, or ness, which means literally a nose, and in this case was a nose of land projecting into a valley – the valley of the Dart, which originally lapped three sides of it. For about a hundred years, from 1750 to 1850, the usual spelling was Totness; then for some reason they reverted to the old orthography.

It was an excellent site, the more so as in Saxon times the river was tidal up to this point and, for boats of shallow draught, navigable. Here the Dart could be forded. And there is still no bridge across it seaward of Totnes. Under Edgar (958–975) the place had its own mint.

In the spring of 1069 William the Conqueror laid siege to Exeter. Before long the whole of the South-West thence to Land's End capitulated without a fight. The lordship of Totnes, and of 107 other manors in Devon, was granted to Judhael, one of William's Breton followers. He erected, at the highest point of the town, a castle of earth and timber: the earthworks were on a big scale. In 1088 he also founded a Priory, as a cell of Angers, which survived until the Dissolution.

A century later the circular keep, which is seventy feet in diameter, was rebuilt in stone, the very coarse stone of this locality. Long ago this region was volcanic, and layers of volcanic ash, deposited in water, ultimately became cemented into solid rocks. That is what this stone is: volcanic ash or tuff. Together with a certain amount of dolerite or 'greenstone', another igneous rock found in association with the tuffs, this is the principal building stone of Totnes. It was quarried on the southern outskirts of the town and just across the river.

There is nothing to see now inside, but the shell of the keep, which was strengthened in 1326, has been carefully restored. Since 1485 it has been used neither as a fortress nor as a residence, but, oddly enough, this Castle, with a bailey on the steep side facing away from the town, has always remained in private ownership. In 1559 it was acquired by the Seymours, and in 1947 the Duke of Somerset transferred it to the care of what was then the Ministry of Works, now the Department of the Environment. Perhaps the principal reason for climbing up the motte today is to enjoy the views from the ramparts.

Totnes acquired walls, but only short sections were ever of stone, as after the Conquest fortifications were not needed here. The rest were merely earth ramparts and fences, or in places just a stout timber palisade. Although it was reconstructed in 1835 with a wider opening, much the best relic of the ancient circuit of walls is the East Gate, half-way up the hill (2, 3).

3. East Gate from High Street in 1929

At the time of Domesday (1086) there were ninety-five houses within the walls and fifteen more outside. By then there was already a wooden bridge over the Dart, which gave place about 1210 to a new one in stone. The bridge, which was less than five feet wide and had eight arches, not all alike, was maintained by a chantry foundation until 1548. Then the Corporation took it over. But even after 1692, when its width was doubled, heavy carts still had to use the fords. The present bridge, of three arches, a fine one in grey Devonian limestone (5) by the Devon-born architect Charles Fowler, was opened in 1828, the year in which he designed his most famous work, Covent Garden Market. Until 1882 a toll had to be paid to cross it.

Prosperity, as usual, depended on trade. Totnes has always been the market town for a rich agricultural district. In the eighteenth century, when half the male population was engaged in farming, that was its chief function. But earlier, various other trades had flourished. One of the first, dating back at least to the twelfth century, was tanning. Percy Russell, the historian of Totnes, recorded that in 1244 the lord of the manor

4. *Totnes from the south, with the Castle in the background*

allowed the Abbot of Torre to purchase sixty hides a year free of toll, in return for two pairs of boots at Michaelmas. Another early industry was slate-quarrying. As long ago as 1180, 800,000 of the local slates were shipped to Winchester, for its Castle. The trade in woollen cloth became important in the thirteenth century, and so did ironwork from the local smithies. There was some ship-building too, and a flourishing trade in meat and fish: under Elizabeth I quantities of pilchards were landed here to be salted and packed into barrels. But as a port Totnes fought a losing battle against Dartmouth. The Dart had to be dredged continually. When, about 1580, Dartmouth embarked upon a highly successful trade in cod, Totnes had no share in it.

Fifty years earlier, principally because of its export trade, Totnes is said to have become the richest town in Devon after Exeter. And the fifteenth century, also a good period, had seen the rebuilding of the Church. The castle has the loftier site, but it is the imposing tower of the church (7) that is the focal point of many a distant view (4). To raise it must have been a formidable undertaking for a town with a population which until a hundred years ago was always well under 4000. It was really due to the energy and enthusiasm of three successive mayors, who, we read, 'drove the townsmen hard'. Some were ordered to go and work in the quarry, which was probably over the hills some miles to the east, near Paignton. For the stone of the tower is not the local tuff but a deep red Permian sandstone, which was brought in barges round the Brixham peninsula and

5. *Totnes Bridge*

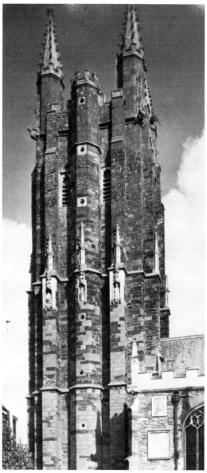

6 *(far left).*
Ashburton
church tower

7 *(left).*
Totnes
church tower

up the Dart to a new quay close to the bridge specially built for it. From there it was dragged up the hill by horses, or perhaps oxen.

We know that in 1450 the overseers had to go and look at four other church towers and to make Totnes 'according to the best model among them', a very typical way of proceeding in the Middle Ages. The tower was evidently a great status symbol. One of the towers specified was Ashburton (6), which has much smaller pinnacles but is otherwise similar in design, although differing in colour and texture because this one is of grey Devonian limestone. Both are striking examples of the Devon type of tower, which hardly occurs outside this county, apart from three in West Somerset. The great feature is the stair turret, often projecting from the middle of one side, usually the south, but at Ashburton the north side. These bold towers with their sweeping lines, strong silhouettes, very small windows and general absence of ornamentation hold a great fascination for some modern architects.

The rest of the church is a mixture of stones, with dark-toned tuffs predominating (8). The red sandstone was used mainly for dressings and for the porch. The gable of the latter and the south aisle parapet, added early in the seventeenth century, are of whitish limestone from Beer in East Devon, which has not worn very well. The Devonian limestone used in the nineteenth century for an additional north aisle is considerably tougher.

With its mainly indifferent pews, hard shiny tiles and poor glass, the interior of this church is no longer very enjoyable. But the screen is still very impressive, and unusual in that it is of stone (also from Beer). When it had its images – in the central part three

8. The Church from the south-east

tiers of small statues under canopies – it must have been wonderful. The loft has gone, but the small coved top which has replaced it provides some compensation for its loss. Parts of the screen have been discreetly recoloured.

Cheek by jowl with the Church, on part of the site of the former Priory, stands the Guildhall (9), a modest little edifice dating from 1553. In the octagonal piers of the arcade we have another local building stone: Dartmoor granite. But there is not much granite in Totnes, for they had so much else, even closer to hand.

Within, there is the Court Room, with the town's coat of arms: a gatehouse crowned by three towers, and flanked by a pair of big keys. Visible under the archway of the gate is a raised portcullis, while in front there is water. Whether this was correct was for long uncertain, but a base *water barry wavy*, as the heralds put it, is now the accepted form. And the river Dart was indeed vital to the prosperity of Totnes. Beyond, in the Council Chamber, the arms occur again, twice in fact, the larger being set between the emblems of Justice and Equity (11). Above runs rather a jolly plaster frieze, with a repeating pattern of prancing winged horses, typically Jacobean (10).

The list of Mayors of the Borough of Totnes – over six hundred of them – goes back to 1359. But alas, Totnes, like all the six towns described in this book, is no longer a borough: it is now only a parish council. It was one of the many victims of the reorganisation of local government in 1974. What a wretched piece of legislation that was! It distorted time-honoured boundaries, ignored history, invented new counties – grotesque creations like Avon and Humberside – and played havoc with civic powers

9. *The Guildhall*

and pride. In my work I disregard it. Bath for me is still in Somerset, Beverley and Hull in the East Riding of Yorkshire. Fortunately Devon was left intact.

Totnes does not now have any houses earlier than the sixteenth century, but quite a number of those in the High Street are of Tudor origin. The main block was usually two rooms thick and three storeys high, the ground floor being set aside for trade.

Underneath one side of the first-floor room a passage ran back into a small courtyard, with a second block beyond, containing the kitchen. Behind this was a long strip of land used for stores and workshops, and also, when there was a back entrance, for stables and pigsties. Where this survives it is now usually a garden. The most complete example is 70 Fore St, a merchant's house of about 1575, which in 1971 was turned into a local museum (12).

Now, although usually no longer very apparent, the fronts of all these Tudor houses, and a good many later ones in the older part of Totnes, are still what they always were: timber-framed. In the course of time the wooden frames with their lath and plaster infilling became masked, sometimes under stucco but often under overcoats of slates, hung upon battens across the front of house after house. The side walls were of the coarse local tuff referred to earlier. But the hung slates on the fronts are the special feature of this town's domestic architecture.

These too were quarried locally: so here is yet one more kind of stone which was at the disposal of the builders of Totnes, and a stone of which they availed themselves unstintingly. The rock is Middle Devonian slate of excellent quality, which splits easily to yield thin slabs suitable not only for hanging vertically but also, of course, for roofing: virtually the whole town is roofed with slate (14).

The quarries, although now much overgrown, can still be identified some three or four miles away to the south-west. A former quarrymen's hut in one of them, now in

13. *53–57 Fore Street*

ruins, shows that this stone can also be used in more massive blocks for building purposes. Given the right conditions this beautiful slate could of course still be worked today, but none of these quarries has in fact supplied Totnes with slate since about the beginning of the present century. If slates are needed here now, they have to be obtained from Delabole, near Camelford in Cornwall. This was the source of the hung slates used in 1927 for a new Post Office, specially designed to fit in with the town – a

14. *Totnes
from the castle*

great credit to the GPO and an ornament to Totnes (16). Would that there were more
contemporary architects willing sometimes to sink their own impulse to design something
which must at all costs look different, and to recognise that there are some situations
where the assertion of too much individuality is just bad manners.

Most of the hung slates in Totnes are merely plain rectangles of varying size (13), but
occasionally they cut their slates into fanciful shapes – spoiling a good many in the
process, no doubt – and hung them to make decorative patterns (15). These fish-scale-
shaped slates are very enjoyable, but at the same time it has to be admitted that
decorative slatework is far more resourceful in both France and Germany than it is here.
In France fish-scale slates on the *tourelles* of *châteaux* are frequently seen, and never fail
to give pleasure. But for slate-hanging at its most brilliant one must go to Hesse, and the
little towns fringing the Harz Mountains. A visit to a town such as Goslar leaves one
wondering whether our own craftsmen in slate have been sufficiently enterprising.

Totnes has a number of examples of polychrome slate-hanging. Generally slates of
contrasting colours were hung in simple horizontal bands, but on the new Civic Hall
they are arranged to make large diamonds. A good many people here paint their slates
(examples are 95–97 (17) and 105 High Street), and this certainly gives the town a more
lively appearance. But I am slightly shocked as a rule by the idea of painting stone; some
of the slates at Totnes are certainly too good to be hidden under paint.

As at Tewkesbury, some of these timber-framed – and here also slate-hung – houses
still retain oak panelling and, especially, plasterwork dating from the Elizabethan and

Opposite:
15 *(top left).*
88 High Street

16 *(top right).*
*The Post Office,
Fore Street*

17 *(right).*
*95–97
High Street*

18 *(far left).*
10 High Street

19 *(left).*
32 High Street

early Stuart periods. At 32 High Street, where there is also a granite chimney-piece (19), which is unusual in this town, the panelling dates from 1577, and there is a ribbed plaster ceiling, with parts of a small frieze too. Other late sixteenth-century ceilings are in the first-floor rooms of No. 10 and 16, a little way lower down the street. The ribs of the Elizabethan ceiling were usually narrow. Under her successor they gradually grew broader. At No. 10 the thin ribs enclose Tudor roses and *fleurs de lis* (18). For motifs like these they would certainly have used moulds. Ribbed ceilings were something of a Devon speciality at this time, and can often be found in quite modest houses. Whether Totnes had its own plasterers is not known, but their chief centres in Devon were at Exeter and Barnstaple.

Jacobean plaster ceilings can be seen at 48 and 64 Fore Street, again in upstairs rooms. The former is mainly floral; the latter, dated 1625, is the finest surviving example in the town (20). The ribs have now become flat bands, and their surfaces are enriched with a tightly-knit running ornament of flowers, fruit, foliage and strapwork. The effect is quite sumptuous. Other motifs include jesters, shells, sprays of oak leaves and pine cones, for all of which they made moulds; for this ceiling they must have had at least twenty different ones. But in two lozenges the relief is bolder, and evidently modelled by hand. One has the Prince of Wales's feathers and the initials CP, so it was done just before Charles I succeeded. In the second lozenge is another representation of the town's coat of arms.

20 *(opposite).*
64 Fore Street

But during the seventeenth century Totnes lost some of its former prosperity, and indeed by 1719 the borough was actually insolvent. A year or two after this Defoe was to declare that, although a good town, it contained more gentlemen than traders. Half the men were now farmers or employed by farmers, and the town was the market for live cattle as well as for their produce. The early eighteenth-century architecture is enjoyable but surprisingly unsophisticated. Nos. 26 and 28 High Street (21), which both date from 1707, provide an amusing contrast. No. 28 (the right-hand one) is decidedly folksy.[1] The other has a poor window in the gable but is the better house. A little farther along the High Street it is not difficult to see that the early Georgian features are only skin-deep, over much earlier timber-framing. Many of the old mullioned casement windows were now replaced by sashes.

The High Street is memorable for its shopping arcades, which used to be known here, a little comically, as the *piazzas*: a misunderstanding of the Italian word for an arcaded square. Today they are called the Butterwalks. There are plenty of these covered walks on the continent: one thinks of Bologna, Padua, Innsbruck and many in France. But, perhaps rather surprisingly in view of our climate, they are not common in England, where only one town has more than Totnes, and that of course is Chester. There the famous Rows run along at first-floor level, and originated, no one knows how, right back in the thirteenth century. Here the earliest appeared in 1584, but in their present form they mostly belong to the eighteenth century. They were achieved by extending the upper floors of existing houses outwards, and supporting their outer corners on piers or pillars, either of wood or granite (22). Though the covered arcade

[1] At the back of this house there was once a small theatre. Hence the three masks on the keystones.

22 *(opposite).*
50–56
High Street

23 *(far left)*.
*Gothick House,
Bank Lane*

24 *(left)*.
47 Fore Street

was welcome, house-owners were also glad to make this alteration because they secured more accommodation. They had therefore to pay an annual charge for encroachment. At one time stalls used to be set up under the arcades, but this of course did not suit the shopkeepers, and was presently prohibited.

Most of the architectural interest of this old town is to be found in one long, steep, narrow and, at the top end, winding street (1), which, even though it has been by-passed and is for one-way traffic only, can still become very much congested. One would like to see parts, if not all, of it become a pedestrian precinct, but for the shopkeepers there are some practical difficulties in the way.

The East Gate separates the upper part, High Street, from the lower part, Fore Street. It is rather a pity that it has been covered with stucco (2, 3). A little below it, up a side alley, is a gem of Gothick: the most entertaining house in Totnes, not least because a public footpath passes right through it! (23) (Incidentally, the back is slate-hung and not Gothick at all.)

Brick made a very late appearance in this town: even in the eighteenth century it was only very sparingly employed. There is one enjoyable little mid-Georgian house in Fore Street, with a Venetian window (24). But the most imposing brick front in Totnes is that of the former King Edward VI Grammar School, built in 1795. The building is otherwise all rubblestone. The doorway has an attractive fanlight, and there is another identical one inside. But until recently the brickwork was almost entirely obscured by a venerable mantle of ivy (25). Happily in November 1983 this was at last removed; but at the time of writing (1984) the building still awaits cleaning and repointing.[1] It should then again become what it was when first erected: a handsome ornament to the town.

25. *The old Grammar School (before the removal of the ivy in 1983)*

Life in Georgian Totnes was genteel and pleasantly unhurried. Visitors all stayed at the Royal Seven Stars (28), which had been built about 1680, with mullioned and transomed windows and without, of course, the present quaint but top-heavy porch, which is early Victorian. But until about 1800 the roads were still very bad and most travellers came on horseback. When at last the condition of the roads improved, the coaches arrived.

About 1830 the 11th Duke of Somerset, the landowner, built another hotel, the Seymour (27), as a rival to the Seven Stars. This is in the suburb of Bridgetown, across the Dart, which was brought within the borough in 1834. Soon after this came a couple of handsome formal terraces, quite unlike anything to be found at Totnes before, or indeed since (26). A good many other houses, especially in the High Street, were refronted about this time, in a search for more architectural dignity and repose.

The South Devon Railway (broad gauge), built by Brunel, was opened from Exeter to Teignmouth in May 1846; to Newton Abbot that December; to Totnes in July 1847;

[1]By 1986 the work was under way but not yet completed.

and on to Plymouth in 1849. This scenically beautiful line, which at Dawlish, hugging the coast, plunges through the same red Permian sandstone as had been used long before for the tower of Totnes church, originally employed the so-called atmospheric system of traction instead of the usual steam engines. Although the large iron air pipe was laid

26. *Devon Place*

27. *Seymour Hotel (closed 1983)*

between the rails nearly as far as Totnes the system never operated beyond Newton Abbot, and in September 1848 had to be abandoned.[1] To many towns railways brought new industry, wealth and, all too often, ugliness. To Totnes it brought none of these. It led to the disappearance of the town's centuries-old river traffic without providing any fresh trade in its place.

So, during the second half of the nineteenth century the population fell from 3828 to 3116, and, apart from a couple of terraces near the station, hardly a single house was built here between about 1840 and 1914, for none was needed. Aesthetically, as I remarked of Tewkesbury, this was a great piece of good fortune for Totnes.

In recent years, however, prosperity has returned: three new industries have arrived, and all appear to be flourishing. A new Civic Hall was erected about 1960, with space for a market below (29). Some of the housing of the last generation is admittedly

[1]The failure was due to various causes, though the story that rats developed a taste for the grease on the leather pipe-valves and even for the leather itself has not been corroborated. The salt sea air presented a problem; and so did the difficulties of co-ordination between the pumping stations in pre-telegraph days.

unworthy, but some is notably good. I would single out two quite dissimilar buildings by the same hand: an older cider warehouse cleverly converted into a residence for elderly retired people, and, on the important river-bank site adjoining the Seymour Hotel, a block of flats interesting for its design and exactly right in scale. This is precisely the sort of place where nowadays some greedy developer, and an architect in league with him, will plead for a high-rise block – and sometimes, heaven knows how, get away with it, and ruin the town. But not here. To build today in an old town without spoiling it is neither easy nor, alas, common, so the architect should be named: he is R. G. Creber.

29. *The Civic Hall*

In 1969 the whole of the old part of Totnes, some seventy acres in all, was, quite rightly, designated as a Conservation Area. An admirable Conservation Study was prepared by the Devon County Council, working in conjunction with the Town. Some of the recommendations have been carried out.

I would not claim that Totnes (which at the last census had 5627 inhabitants) is one of the most beautiful of our small towns. But it is certainly one of the most distinctive. And the preservation of that individuality is vital.

LUDLOW

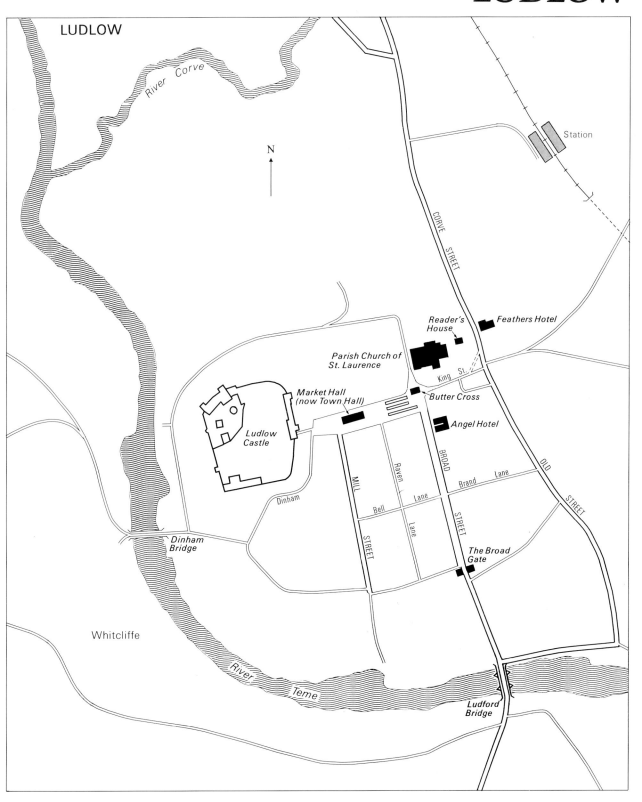

LUDLOW

River Corve

N

Station

CORVE STREET

Reader's House

Feathers Hotel

Parish Church of St. Laurence

King St.

Market Hall (now Town Hall)

Butter Cross

Ludlow Castle

Angel Hotel

Dinham

MILL STREET

Raven Lane

Bell Lane

BROAD STREET

Brand Lane

OLD STREET

Dinham Bridge

The Broad Gate

Whitcliffe

River Teme

Ludford Bridge

1. *Ludlow – town plan*

2. *Isaac Vogelsanck's* Prospect of Ludlow, *1772*

3. *Ludlow from Whitcliffe*

Ludlow, like Richmond, was a Norman creation, although, also like Richmond, it does not occur in Domesday Book. The Conqueror had granted the large manor of Stanton to one of his stalwart supporters, Walter de Lacy, and entrusted him with the special responsibility of guarding that part of the English border against the still unconquered Welsh. And the village of Stanton Lacy is still very much there, three miles away to the north.

Although documentary evidence is lacking, it would seem that about 1090, in order the better to carry out his assignment, Walter's son, Roger de Lacy, decided to build a castle. Not unnaturally, he chose to locate it at the most easily defensible point on his lands. One excellent site he had: a cliff which on three sides drops steeply towards rivers – to the Teme on the south and west and, on the north side, to its tributary the Corve. So here was placed what, in the course of time, became a truly splendid castle (6).

The Castle stands on the stone of which most of it was built: a rough, chunky, calcareous siltstone of the Silurian age. The still surviving dry moat between the outer and inner baileys'shows where some of it was hacked out. The other stone used here was Old Red sandstone, which was probably brought from a quarry a mile or so away to the east. It can be masoned in a way that is impossible with the Silurian stone.

Only on one side, the east, was the site vulnerable, and this was the side which faced away from Wales, Here, protected by its walls, arose the town. The Normans built it, but, just as at Totnes, the name derives from two Anglo-Saxon words: *low*, meaning a hill, and *lud*, 'by the loud waters'.

Again, like Richmond, the town came into being in the first instance to serve the needs of the castle. But the surrounding lands were much more fertile here than up in Swaledale, and Ludlow soon became a flourishing market town for the surrounding district. By 1200 it already had its grammar school. Trade thrived too, especially wool, and, before long, cloth-making. The cloth trade was bringing prosperity to this town as early as the thirteenth century, and Stokesay Castle, a few miles to the north-west, was built about 1270 by the son of a Ludlow clothier.

The much larger Castle of Ludlow belongs to three distinct periods. The Chapel (4) is Norman. Its chancel has gone, but the nave, apart from its roof, survives. It was circular, which was something of a rarity in England: there are now only four others,[1] although the foundations of five more are known. Both the doorway and the chancel arch have profuse zig-zag decoration. Norman also was the now-blocked gatehouse, enlarged shortly before 1200 to form the Keep.

Then there is the Great Hall (5). This was built by the Mortimers, who got the Castle by marriage in 1307, when the male Lacy line petered out. While retaining the for-

[1] Northampton, Cambridge, the Temple Church in London and Little Maplestead in Essex. All were inspired by the Church of the Holy Sepulchre at Jerusalem, and the first two carry that dedication.

tifications, they promptly set about converting the place into a fine house. The main hall, which in 1634 saw the first performance of Milton's *Comus*, was upstairs. Its floor was carried on huge beams. For the early fourteenth century, this was an unusually splendid hall. It only became ruinous in the reign of George II, when unhappily the order was given to strip off and sell the lead from the roof.

In 1475 Ludlow was chosen as the seat of the Council of the Marches, set up to govern

Wales and the Border. The Castle became the residence of the President of the Council. For part of the reign of Elizabeth I he was Sir Henry Sidney, father of Sir Philip, the soldier poet. It was he who added, in 1581, the pleasantly domestic-looking building to the right of the entrance to the inner bailey. The Council was not finally abolished until 1689. It was only then that the Castle became, in a word much in use today, redundant. It has never belonged to the town; the present owner is the Earl of Powis.

Daniel Defoe came to Ludlow about 1723, and has left us this picture:

> The situation of this castle is most beautiful. . . . It only wants the residence of its princes, but that is not now to be expected. The castle itself is in the very perfection of decay. All the five courts, the royal apartments, halls, and rooms of state lie open, abandoned, and some of them falling down; for since the Courts of the President and Marches are taken away, there is nothing to do that requires the attendance of any public people. So time, that great devourer of the works of man, begins to eat into the stone walls, and to spread the face of royal ruins upon the whole fabric.

But in our own time, thanks to an ambitiously planned annual Festival, the Castle, for a fortnight every summer, bubbles with life again. Few theatrical producers can aspire to

5. The Great Hall

6. *The Castle from below*

so spectacular a setting as this courtyard, particularly as the daylight fades and the floodlights take over.

Because of its lofty site and the height of its tower, the parish church, St Laurence, is an even more commanding feature of Ludlow's skyline (2, 3). It is the largest church in Shropshire, and the proudest. Like so many others, it was built by the townspeople ('Ludlovians'), mainly in the fifteenth century, when this place was just about at the zenith of its prosperity. There were guilds for many trades: mercers, stitchmen (among whom were the drapers), shoemakers, fletchers or arrow-makers, millers, butchers, fishmongers and, above all, wool-merchants and clothiers. The fletchers provided the north transept: their badge is still to be seen on the roof. But it was primarily the profits of the wool trade which paid for this building; it was one of a good many English parish churches which, as the old saying had it, were built on the backs of sheep.

The church is mainly built of Old Red sandstone, which, it may be worth remarking, is by no means always red. It has undergone a great deal of restoration. Nevertheless, there are some notable features here. Externally, besides the tower, there is the hexagonal South porch, which is one of the only two in England of this shape.[1]

[1] The other, much richer, is at St Mary Redcliffe, Bristol.

The interior looks almost wholly Perpendicular. It is stately and finely proportioned, yet, like so many town churches, not very lovable. The stained glass is frequently overpraised; it was never very distinguished, and has been much restored. The best features are in oak. The tall nave has a handsome tie-beam roof with carved bosses, and under the central tower, lit by windows above the tower arches, is a roof which is not sumptuous but has great charm (7). Admittedly it is a stone design carried out in wood, but so is the roof of the Octagon at Ely, and who but the most strait-laced pedant could fault either of them?

The superstructure of the stalls is mostly Victorian, but the seats are original, and they harbour one of the best sets of parochial misericords (although not all of one date) in the country. The appeal of misericords is by no means always primarily artistic. This is true here, for example, of the popular kitchen scene, which shows the cook on a low chair, a big kettle and a couple of pigs ready for the spit. (It has been suggested that this stands for one of the Occupations of the Months: January, perhaps. But Ludlow does not have any others in that series.) And, accomplished as they are, it is first and foremost for their social interest that we enjoy the scholar, the (now headless) wrestlers and the tapster: the only known example of this subject on a misericord (8). Others include heraldic allusions: one has the chained antelope of Henry VI (9); another the falcon and

fetterlock which was the badge of Richard, Duke of York (10), who got the lordship of Ludlow when his brother became King Edward V; a third has the Prince of Wales's feathers (11), serving to recall the close associations which Ludlow has always had with Wales.

But some of these misericords are real works of art, crisply carved, uncrowded, and decorative. Among my favourites are the three women's head-dresses (12), the hart and two hounds (13), the owl and two birds (14), and, best of all, the mermaid between two fishes: a little masterpiece of suave design (15).

In the churchyard there is not a gravestone to be seen. This will distress some people and delight others: it is a highly controversial, and indeed emotive, subject. Most people who are deeply concerned about the future of our churches are highly critical of the modern predilection for churchyard clearance, and scornful of the 'tidy' churchyard as something at best suburban or municipal and at worst an offence against history and an irreverence to the dead, to say nothing of its harmful effects upon the maintenance of wildlife. I do not always share this indignation, and I feel I should explain why.

There are of course many English churchyards of surpassing charm, which are a great enhancement to the church. Remote country churches that seem to leap out of the long grass or float upon a sea of cow parsley are a delight, and here nothing should be changed. Rural churchyards are sometimes cropped by sheep, and this too is acceptable, despite the wire fences which have to be installed temporarily. But in all these churchyards the gravestones will normally be of English, and often of the local, stone; and this consideration is vital.

Tombstones scarcely appeared outside the church before the seventeenth century and remained rare until the eighteenth. Then there was a profuse outburst. It is safe to say that all our best gravestones without exception are Georgian, always notable for their fine lettering and often for scrolls and cherubic angels and other carvings in addition. Here and there are large chest-tombs and, in the Cotswolds, bale tombs, recalling some of the prosperous families of wool merchants on whose bounty these churches so often depended. The stone for these tombs is invariably English, and never are there either kerbs or chips. These are dignified memorials and, although the inscriptions are now sometimes indecipherable, they always give pleasure. Only where they are in a state of irremediable decay is their removal justified.

About the middle of the nineteenth century there was an abrupt change. The transportation of heavy stones from afar, which up to this time had been difficult, suddenly became easy and relatively inexpensive. As a consequence, the country was flooded with memorials from distant places: screaming white marbles from Italy, polished pink granites from Aberdeen, pepper-and-salt granites from Cornwall, shiny blacks too, and various other totally inappropriate materials. Firms of monumental masons now sprouted everywhere, and it was they who recommended these alien stones,

8

9

10

11

12

13

14

15

8–15. *Misericords in St Laurence's Church*

both on account of their cheapness and because of their undeniable durability. The Victorian age was one of rapidly rising population and of people who made something of a cult of death and of mourning. It was therefore not long before the churchyards were invaded, and some well nigh overwhelmed, by what in general were purely commercial products. In some places, where the incumbent or the diocesan advisory authorities have little aesthetic appreciation or are lax about exercising their discretion, these memorial stones have done – and are still doing – appalling damage, visually, to the setting of many a fine church that has done nothing to deserve such improprieties.

These are the gravestones which I would like to see photographed, recorded, and then removed, until not a single one is left in a churchyard throughout the length and breadth of the land. The designs are usually debased, the lettering commonplace, the inscriptions banal and the materials themselves an offence. A churchyard is a communal burial ground, and also a public place, potentially to be enjoyed by everyone. There can surely be no individual right, either legal or moral, to ignore the general good in the pursuit of personal preference, by erecting memorials of this kind.

The maintenance of our churchyards also poses great problems. Village churchyards, notably in favoured areas like the Cotswolds, may be lovingly cared for, often, one suspects, by public-spirited local volunteers, but even when they are unkempt there are compensations, especially for naturalists. Towns are quite different. A neglected town churchyard is hardly ever acceptable, and often an eyesore. Clearances should usually depend upon the quality of the memorials, most of which are no longer tended by any member of the family commemorated. Georgian gravestones can sometimes with advantage be moved, although never to make a low wall round the periphery of the churchyard, but, together with all those in the local or in some other appropriate English stone, should not be eliminated unless in a serious state of decay. Foreign and artificial stones should be removed as quickly as possible; and, above all, no more should under any circumstances be allowed. Kerbs should also be prohibited.

I differ from some people in feeling that, if in some places this results in no tombstones being left, it is a cause for regret. A broad expanse of mown lawn always enhances the dignity of a large town church, just as it does of a country house or a college quadrangle, whereas even good memorials, placed around a church of this kind, are inevitably puny in scale. In some towns, moreover, the resulting open space provides a valuable 'lung' in what may otherwise be a heavily built-up area. And in towns the memorials often tend to be seriously smoke-begrimed. In short, each churchyard has to be considered on its merits (or demerits), and treated accordingly.

The clearance of the churchyard at Ludlow was carried out in memory of a former rector. It is not an altogether good example, because the lawn is absolutely flat and a railing shuts it off from the church itself; moreover, some good memorials may have been sacrificed here. But some of my friends wax so indignant whenever they see a cleared churchyard that I have felt it necessary to plead for a more balanced approach to this difficult problem. If for emotional or other reasons there are people who still want white marble or artificial stone or chips of adulterated *crème-de-menthe* green, let them be directed to those abodes of visual desolation, the municipal cemeteries.

The Castle and the Church are built of stone, but not much else is at Ludlow, except the bridges. There are three of these, and all are good. Down the hill to the south, the Teme was bridged here as long ago as the twelfth century. The present Ludford Bridge (16), with its big bold cut-waters, belongs mainly to the fifteenth century. The other two bridges are Georgian. Dinham Bridge, of 1823, is the third on this site: it also crosses the Teme. The Corve Bridge, of about 1789, is smaller, but very distinctive, with its semi-elliptical arches.

Ludlow from the outset was a planned town, which in the Middle Ages was fairly unusual. It had a grid plan: and, except at one corner, where the grid was disrupted when the Outer Bailey of the Castle was extended about 1200, most of it still survives, within the crumbling remains of what were once the Town Walls (1, 17).

One street, the spine of the town, runs east from the Castle along the crest of the hill. This, appropriately enough, is High Street. Originally it was wide, but later it became partly filled in by the Market Hall and a number of parallel lanes to the east of it.

From this spine a number of straight streets spill down the hill towards the river. Two of them, Mill Street and Broad Street, are still unusually wide for so small a town, and, although today they look Georgian, there seems little doubt that in medieval times

16. *Ludford Bridge*

these two streets were just as broad as they are now. Mill Street is handsome: Broad Street is unforgettable – indeed, one of the best in England. Here, half-way down, is the sole survivor of Ludlow's six thirteenth-century gatehouses; and perched on top, with complete confidence, is a capacious eighteenth-century house (18, 19).

Beyond the Broad Gate the road continues downhill. The gradient here used to be precipitous but Thomas Telford, whom we met at Mythe Bridge outside Tewkesbury, and who was the County Surveyor for Shropshire, eased it by making an embankment.

17. *Plan of Ludlow, 1835*

18, 19. *The Broad Gate from the south and from the north*

20

21

22

23

Broad Street. The watercolour (20) by Louise Rayner, c. 1850, shows the Butter Cross much as it is today (22). An old (c. 1900) photograph (21) of the east side of Broad Street shows the Angel, which also appears on the far right of the recent photograph (23) of the same side of the street looking south.

Until about 1700 virtually every house in the town was timber-framed. Plenty of stone was available, but there was an abundance of oak too, and to build with wood was a lot cheaper. As at Tewkesbury, a considerable number of these old timber-framed buildings still survive. But a couple of centuries ago the oak frames might well have seemed to be less in evidence than they are now. Compare, for example, the top end of Broad Street even as it looked about 1900 and as it is today (21, 23). The fact is that the Georgians did not really like exposed timbers, any more than on churches they approved of flying buttresses: propriety, they felt, demanded that both should be masked. Nowadays a great array of exposed framing always wins many admirers.

What is certain is that the men who built these houses, largely in the years between 1560 and 1640 but in certain cases earlier, did not for a moment intend that their oak should be hidden behind whitewash or plaster. For, if this were the intention, why go to such trouble in producing decorative patterns? Now and again, admittedly, they overdid it. There is one building in Broad Street which evokes nothing so much as a visit to the oculist. But all those diamond-shaped lozenges, sometimes with concave sides, which might even be cusped or spiked, or contrived as lozenges within lozenges – were they done for structural reasons? Obviously not. The mood is one of ebullient display (22, 23, 24), and these fronts were intended to be seen.

So also with the carved oak consoles or brackets (25), which would seem to have been something of a Ludlow speciality. In some of them the carvers were enjoying themselves enormously, and there can be no doubt that they wanted to share their pleasure.

But the 'black and white' still characteristic not only of Ludlow but of the West country in general dates only from the Victorian period. In recent years, at Ludlow as at

*26 (opposite).
The Reader's
House*

Tewkesbury (see p. 81), some efforts have been made – and very welcome they are – to de-black the oak and restore it to its natural colour. This can be seen at the Reader's House (the Reader was one of the Rector's assistants) on the east side of the churchyard, where in 1616 a picturesque double-jettied addition in oak and plaster was fitted on to the rubblestone front of a much earlier building (26). Still more strikingly can it be seen at the Feathers Hotel, built in 1603. Anyone who remembers this a few years ago, sticky black all over, can hardly fail to be delighted by the change (27).

The Feathers is Ludlow's most famous timber-framed building, and certainly its most riotously exuberant. It has been a good deal restored: neither the balcony nor the inscription are original, and the entrance has been moved. But the front door (28) is old, with its ornamental lock-plate, two very long hinges, and no fewer than 305 iron studs. (Not hearsay, because I counted them!) The interior is no less rich, especially the panelled room upstairs with an ornate plaster ceiling and a big carved overmantel of oak with panels of marquetry and the coat of arms of James I (29). A room on the ground floor has the carved arms of William III.

Towards the end of the seventeenth century Ludlow lost some of its former prosperity. Defoe wrote: 'The town declineth. . . . It was formerly a place of good trade.' But happily the decline was only temporary, a fact to which the wealth of good Georgian houses bears ample witness. These are nearly all of brick, and there were several

28, 29. *The Feathers Hotel, front door and James I room*

brickworks in the vicinity: one, indeed, hardly a mile from the town centre. The appearance of the town was much altered, and in my view greatly improved, during the eighteenth century. The new affluence was partly due to the starting of another industry: glove-making, which, during the Napoleonic wars when French competition was removed, did very well indeed.

Ludlow also became, in Georgian days, a social centre for the surrounding nobility and gentry: people like the Earl of Powis, the Knight family from Downton Castle, and the Salways, squires of Richards Castle. The condition of the roads was so bad that, especially in winter, these people were reluctant to travel to and fro from their country estates, even when, as with the Salways, these were not far distant. Other houses, no less pleasing, were the homes of professional men or local merchants.

There is hardly a street in the town without these gracious Georgian houses. Occasionally, it is true, people's enthusiasm ran away with them, to produce architectural solecisms such as would never have occurred closer to London. There is the house with the Venetian windows, for example. This kind of window – so difficult to find in Venice, by the way – was a favourite motif in our Georgian architecture, often employed for a staircase, or for the two end rooms of a symmetrical elevation. But whoever would have thought of having Venetian windows and nothing else? Eight of them (31). A prize example, to be sure, of over-egging the pudding!

32. *Samuel Scott,*
Broad Street,
Ludlow, *c. 1760*

In general, though, the quality is high, especially in Mill Street and, above all, Broad Street.[1] Such typically Georgian features as moulded, wooden pilastered doorcases, wrought-iron fanlights and wooden modillioned eaves are much in evidence, and nearly all the sash-framed windows happily keep their glazing bars. Some are set under flat arches of rubbed brick. Here and there a house is bounded by plain brick pilasters. A pleasant feature of Broad Street is the cobbled inclines between road and pavements, valiantly fought for and saved a few years ago when it was proposed to remove them. Near the gatehouse these now culminate in a wrought-iron railing at the pavement's edge (19). The house-fronts here are practically faultless, and Broad Gate House itself provides a fascinating study in Georgian window design, with the oldest window, not blocked later but constructed as a dummy, in the centre at the top (19).

This must be one of our most original houses in its siting. The livery is now grey, and a great success: a most elegant addition to this marvellous street. It was from one of the windows of this house that, about 1760, Samuel Scott did his painting, looking straight

30 *(far left).*
A view in
Mill Street

31 *(left).*
39 Broad Street

[1] The year 1979 saw the publication (by Studio Press, Birmingham) of *Broad Street: its houses and residents throughout eight centuries*, written by David Lloyd on behalf of the Ludlow Historical Research Group, and beautifully illustrated by Stanley Woolston. There can hardly be a street in England that is now as fully documented in all its aspects, and scarcely one that better deserves to be.

34. *27 Broad Street* up the street to the Butter Cross at the top (32). Except for the pervasive motor vehicles, the scene since then has changed very little.

The Butter Cross (22, 33), set up in 1743–6, is one of Ludlow's comparatively few stone buildings. The style is Classical with just a touch of the Baroque: its architect was William Baker from Audlem in Cheshire. The stone continues up to the clock turret, with inverted consoles to each side, but the octagonal cupola is of wood. This carries a tiny dome, ball finial and weather-vane. The upper room was originally intended as a town hall. Later it harboured a charity school; now it is a small museum. The Butter Cross is not a subtle building, but it is a great ornament to the town.

Broad Street has one house, and a very handsome one, built of stone: No. 27 (34). It looks as if the surface of this rather rough stone, which could never have been ashlared, was scored in readiness for a coat of stucco. In fact, stucco was never intended. This house was originally built of the local Silurian limestone, probably quarried on Whitcliffe, about 1685. The elegant porch and other refinements were added in 1764. But the stone decayed, and by 1956 was in a crumbling condition. The only practicable course was to chip off the surface to a depth of about an inch, and waterproof it; and this

33 *(opposite).*
The Butter Cross
from the east side

is what was done. Within, there is one charming mid-eighteenth-century fireplace and an elegant staircase. Like many others in Ludlow, this house had a large walled garden at the back, and in the garden was erected an enchanting gazebo, which is now in separate ownership (39). Although only cement on brick, it is finished with battlements and a wrought-iron weather-vane. It commands a view of the hills beyond the Teme.

The preponderance of brick and timber-framing in Ludlow is highlighted by the fact that in Corve Street there is a building called Stone House. Erected late in the eighteenth century, it is indeed of stone, homely rubblestone, but this is not apparent from the front, which was put on about 1840 and is of stucco (36). This front is undeniably imposing, even grand, but it is also out of scale (35) and decidedly pompous, and one cannot feel that it has anything to do with Ludlow.

Unhappily there was much worse to come. Among my friends are a few who are wont to chide me for sometimes being a shade unjust to Victorian buildings (and it is true that

35. *Corve Street, looking south*

I am quite unaffected by the current vogue for them), but it is hard to find a good, even a bearable, Victorian building in Ludlow. Sir Nikolaus Pevsner was for many years Chairman of the Victorian Society, so it is fair to quote from his *Shropshire* volume (the more so as he dedicated it to me!). In Broad Street there is the Methodist Church, Italianate of 1878, 'a painful jog' for the array of Georgian properties which surround it. In King St there is 'one Victorian abomination': No. 18. Then there is No. 1, Dinham, 'a High Victorian shocker, of multi-coloured brick with a timber-framed gable too tall to be in scale – and at the very corner of Castle Square'. And finally, worst of all because so obtrusively prominent, there is the Town Hall (37), built in 1887 as the Market Hall, by Henry A. Cheers of Twickenham. 'Ludlow's bad luck', Pevsner called it. 'There is

38. *Louise Rayner's watercolour of c. 1850, showing the Old Market Hall*

nothing that could be said in favour of its fiery brick or useless Elizabethan detail.' Yet a drawing preserved in the Museum reveals that about 1880 they sought to replace the Old Market Hall by something even more florid! The painting of about 1850 by Louise Rayner, also in the Museum, shows what the present building replaced (38).

Yet, all things considered, it is wonderful how little this old town has changed. Another mid-nineteenth-century painting by Louise Rayner from the top of Broad Street may aptly be compared with the same view today (20, 22).

The only way to see a town properly is on foot. Ludlow is small enough to get to know intimately, just by walking about. There is a delightful mixture of building materials, all of local provenance. Stone from nearby quarries, and some of it from the very rock upon which this town stands; bricks baked from the local clays; oaks from the forests. No exposed concrete at all, because concrete, however useful structurally, belongs nowhere. Wherever these local materials are used, with a proper sense of scale, all is well.

Nothing has contributed more to the preservation of Ludlow than the construction, a few years back, of a by-pass road. This involved building, a mile or so to the south-east, a new bridge over the Teme. It has been infinitely worth it. No longer do the heavy lorries thunder through streets quite unsuited to carry them. Ludlow is a working town, and not by any means a fossilised museum piece, but the new road has rendered it a great deal more enjoyable for residents and visitors alike.

39. Gazebo in garden of 5 Brand Lane

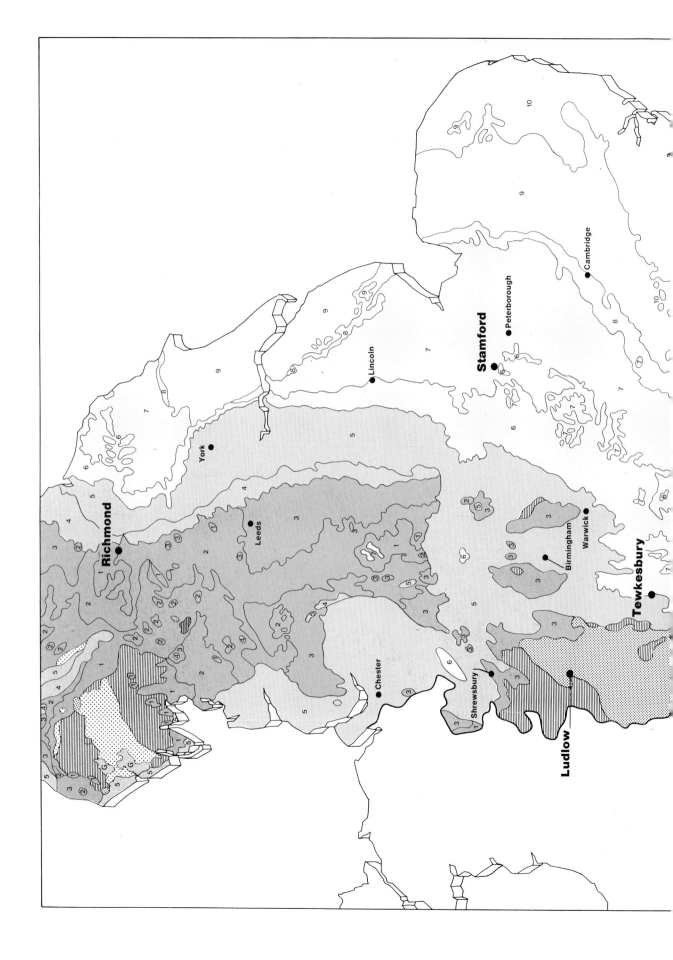

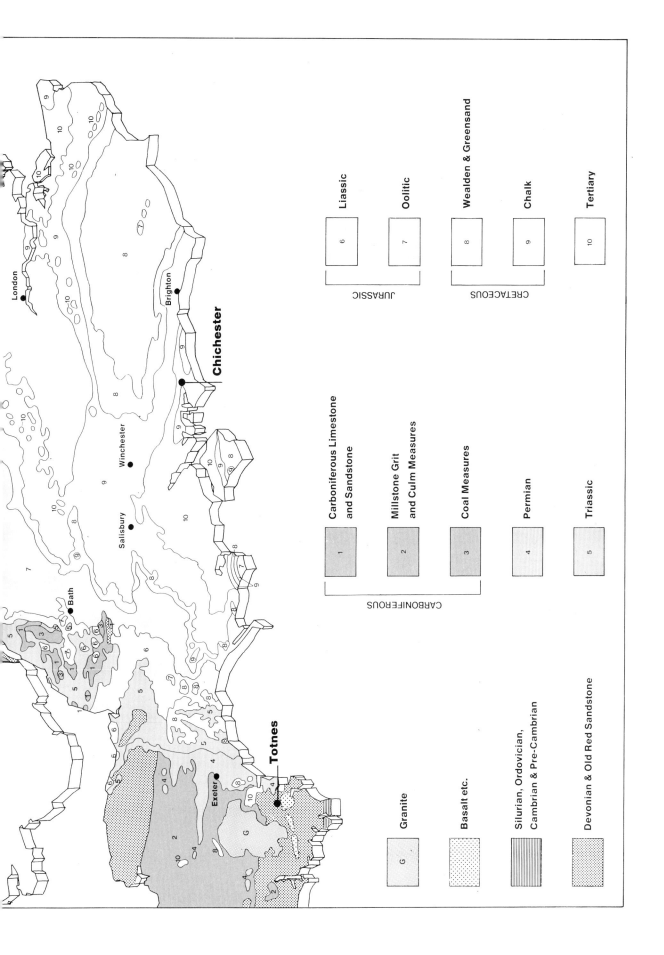

London

Brighton

Chichester

Winchester

Salisbury

Bath

Totnes

Exeter

CARBONIFEROUS

1	Carboniferous Limestone and Sandstone
2	Millstone Grit and Culm Measures
3	Coal Measures
4	Permian
5	Triassic

JURASSIC

6	Liassic
7	Oolitic

CRETACEOUS

8	Wealden & Greensand
9	Chalk
10	Tertiary

G	Granite
	Basalt etc.
	Silurian, Ordovician, Cambrian & Pre-Cambrian
	Devonian & Old Red Sandstone

PICTURE CREDITS

The photographs in this book, apart from those listed below, were taken by Geoff Howard and reproduced from prints made by Michael Spry of Downtown Darkrooms.

Acknowledgement is due to the following for permission to reproduce illustrations: Aerofilms, p. 12; BBC pp. 144 top, 165, 166; Friends of Ludlow Museum, p. 168 bottom; Georgian Theatre, Richmond, p. 59; A.F. Kersting, p. 48 top; National Monuments Record, pp. 15, 16, 17, 45, 56, 66, 80 right (copyright Oxford City Library), 82, 97 top, 104 right, 112, 122, 124 (copyright B.T. Batsford); Salop County Museum Service, pp. 154, 156 top, 163; Margaret Sims, p. 115 right; Sussex Archaeological Trust, p. 42; *Torquay Herald Express*, p. 138 left; Usher Art Gallery, Lincoln, p. 97 bottom. The town plans on pp. 11, 43, 67, 93, 121 and 143 were drawn by ESR Ltd, cartographers.